NOTABLE IMAGES OF VIRTUE

Notable Images
of Virtue

Emily Brontë, George Meredith, W. B. Yeats

BEING THE SIXTH SERIES OF LECTURES
ON THE CHANCELLOR DUNNING TRUST LECTURES
DELIVERED AT QUEEN'S UNIVERSITY,
KINGSTON, ONTARIO, 1954

C. DAY LEWIS

Professor of Poetry, University of Oxford

FOLCROFT LIBRARY EDITIONS / 1974

Library of Congress Cataloging in Publication Data

Day-Lewis, Cecil, 1904-1972.
    Notable images of virtue: Emily Brontë, George
Meredith, W. B. Yeats.

    Reprint of the ed. published by Ryerson Press, Toronto,
issued as one of the Chancellor Dunning Trust lectures,
delivered at Queen's University, Kingston, Ontario, 1954.
    1. English poetry--19th century--Addresses, essays,
lectures. I. Title. II. Series: Kingston, Ont.
Queen's University. Chancellor Dunning Trust. Lectures,
1954.
PR583.D3 1974   820'.9'008   74-3179
ISBN 0-8414-5724-7 (lib. bdg.)

Limited 100 Copies

Manufactured in the United States of America

Folcroft Library Editions
Box 182
Folcroft, Pa. 19032

Notable Images
of Virtue

Emily Brontë, George Meredith, W. B. Yeats

BEING THE SIXTH SERIES OF LECTURES
ON THE CHANCELLOR DUNNING TRUST LECTURES
DELIVERED AT QUEEN'S UNIVERSITY,
KINGSTON, ONTARIO, 1954

C. DAY LEWIS

Professor of Poetry, University of Oxford

The Ryerson Press — Toronto

Published May, 1954

PRINTED AND BOUND IN CANADA
BY THE RYERSON PRESS, TORONTO

ACKNOWLEDGMENTS

The quotations from *Collected Poems, Reveries Over Childhood and Youth, Ideas of Good and Evil,* and *The Cutting of an Agate,* by W. B. Yeats, are reprinted by permission of Mrs. W. B. Yeats and the Macmillan Company of Canada, Ltd. The quotations from *W. B. Yeats,* by Joseph Hone, are reprinted by permission of Macmillan and Co., Ltd., London, who are also the British publishers of Yeats' poetry and prose.

The quotations from *The Poetical Works of George Meredith* are reprinted by permission of Messrs. Constable and Co., Ltd.

The quotations from *The Poetry of W. B. Yeats,* by Louis MacNeice (Oxford University Press) are reprinted by permission of the author.

The quotation from L. A. G. Strong's essay on W. B. Yeats, in *Personal Remarks,* is reprinted by permission of the author and Peter Nevill Ltd.

The quotation from Philip Henderson's Introduction to his edition of *The Poems of Emily Brontë* is reprinted by permission of the author and The Folio Society Ltd.

The quotations from *The Brontë Story,* by Margaret Lane, are reprinted by permission of the author and William Heinemann Ltd.

I am grateful to Macmillan and Co., Ltd., for permission to incorporate material from my essay on W. B. Yeats, which appeared in *Scattering Branches*; and to Rupert Hart-Davis for permission to incorporate material from my Introduction to his edition of *Modern Love.*

Acknowledgment is also made to the authors and publishers for the use of quotations from Fannie Elizabeth Ratchford's *The Brontës' Web of Childhood,* published by the Columbia University Press, and from Edmund Wilson's *Axel's Castle,* published by Charles Scribner's Sons.

To
ENID STARKIE

FOREWORD

THE PURPOSE of the Chancellor Dunning Trust, established at Queen's University in 1948, is "to promote understanding and appreciation of the supreme importance of the dignity, freedom and responsibility of the individual person in human society." It is laid down in the conditions of the Trust that the Trustees of the University shall every three years determine the means by ·which the purposes of the Trust shall be pursued. For the present the method selected has been an annual series of lectures given at the University during the academic session. The pattern established has been three formal lectures accompanied by a considerable number of informal talks and discussions with students and staff.

There have now been six series of these lectures. For the first three years, distinguished lecturers examined the philosophic bases of liberty. During the second period of three years, equally distinguished lecturers have pursued the theme through the fields of history, political philosophy and literature.

The selection of lecturers has not in any country been reduced to an exact art. The University was particularly happy in the selection of the sixth lecturer. C. Day Lewis, Professor of Poetry at Oxford, is easily identified as a distinguished poet; that he is also an accomplished and forceful lecturer has now been verified by our experience. That he would be able to convey to undergraduates something of the importance of poetry was an ideal for which we could only hope until he had brilliantly realized it.

It is a pleasure to know that these lectures are now available in this form to a wider audience. I regret only that many of the readers of this little volume had not the opportunity of hearing the fine reading of poetry which was part of the lectures.

W. A. MACKINTOSH
Vice-Chancellor and Principal.

Queen's University at Kingston,
March 31, 1954.

PREFACE

PHILIP SIDNEY said it was the poet's task to "feign," that is, to compose, "notable images of virtue." The Chancellor Dunning Trust lectures are directed towards "the dignity, freedom and responsibility of the individual person in human society." In my lectures I tried to approach and illuminate these great human virtues through the writings of three poets to whom they were of paramount concern. The approach and the illumination, since it is poetry I am dealing with, are necessarily oblique; but not, I hope, less valuable for this reason than the more direct contributions which can be made by the historian, the philosopher or the sociologist. My immediate subjects—Emily Brontë, George Meredith, W. B. Yeats—were all poets: and poets "are of imagination all compact"; and the imagination, said Shelley, "is the greatest instrument of moral good."

I am deeply sensible of the honour done me by the Trustees of the Chancellor Dunning Trust, in asking me to give these lectures. I would like to say how grateful I am to the Vice-Chancellor and Principal, Dr. W. A. Mackintosh, and to Faculty members and students of the University, for the innumerable kindnesses which made my visit as great a pleasure as a privilege: there can surely be no University where a stranger is made to feel more quickly and thoroughly at home, or finds more stimulating company. With the opportunities he has for making such varied personal contacts, for learning no less than for teaching, the Dunning Trust lecturer is lucky indeed.

C. DAY LEWIS.

xi

CONTENTS

xiii

I

EMILY BRONTË AND FREEDOM

FREEDOM: dignity: responsibility. They are big words—
big words and rather overpowering ideas. A historian or
a philosopher can grapple with the ideas; a propagandist
can learn to say the words: but for the poet, for the
literary critic, the approach to these great abstractions
must be oblique, wary, empirical. Poetry itself, so far as
we can discover a general law valid for all its diverse
manifestations, is a movement from the particular to the
universal, from the concrete to the abstract. A poem is a
stone dropped into a pool: its waves go rippling and
fading concentrically outwards, the impression it makes on
the pool, on us, depending upon the size of the stone and
the imaginative height from which it has fallen. The business of the poem is to set up that initial disturbance: what
may happen afterwards is not its business, for a poem is
not there to prove anything or convert anyone. Nevertheless, its effects may be considerable: those concentric rings
travel far from the point of impact; and although, a
minute later, the face of the pool is again a sleeping face,
its depths may have been stirred—as the pool of Bethesda
was stirred by an angel's wing.

And so it is with the poet. He may think as hard or
feel as passionately as anyone else about freedom, responsibility, human dignity. But such thoughts and feelings,
when he composes a poem, must be controlled—subordina-
ted and subdued to the task in hand, which is a task, not
of preaching or persuasion, but of creating an imaginative

1

object. A poem, for example, will not give us a statement about freedom so much as an image of freedom—an image created by the fusion of feeling with thought. A poet will write about a caged bird, and through this image animate for us the idea of freedom—bring it to life as no amount of statistics, no wealth of argument, no array of rhetorical apostrophizings can do. The poet who writes that poem has worked from the particular to the universal: his inward eye has been fastened, not upon the abstraction of liberty, but upon a bird in a cage; this bird, if all goes well with the poem, sings for all prisoners and captives, utters its protest against the limitations of our human nature. The stone has dropped, the rings of meaning move outwards, wider and wider.

Poets, of course, have their ruling passions—themes to which their poetry is constantly returning. In these lectures I am going to talk about three poets, each of whom, I believe, can enlighten us on one aspect of our three-fold subject. W. B. Yeats was much preoccupied with the idea of human dignity; George Meredith, in *Modern Love,* was absorbed by the problems of individual responsibility: Emily Brontë was all her life consumed by a passion for freedom. Today I will discuss Emily Brontë's work. Not only does it illuminate the idea of freedom; but it is also a classic example of the way poetry moves from the particular to the universal, and the way so much poetry is "a harvest from small beginnings." The beginnings of her work and her sisters' could hardly have been smaller or more concrete. *Jane Eyre, Wuthering Heights,* and Emily Brontë's poems all started from a box of toy soldiers.

On June 5th, 1826, Rev. Patrick Brontë brought back from Leeds, for his son Branwell, a box of wooden soldiers. At this date Emily was nearly eight years old. The soldiers were used at first for war games, representing

Napoleon and his marshals, Wellington and his staff. Presently they were transformed into characters, historical or imaginary, in a saga invented by Charlotte and Branwell, added to daily, continued even after the two elder children had grown up. This saga, the story of an imaginary country called Angria, was written down in microscopic handwriting in a series of small notebooks, which were virtually ignored by Brontë scholars and biographers till, some hundred years later, Miss Fannie Elizabeth Ratchford examined and deciphered them, and in her book *The Brontës' Web of Childhood*, showed how widely Charlotte drew upon the saga of Angria for the characters and incidents of her works.

When Emily Brontë was in her early teens, she and Anne broke away from this game in which all the children had played, and set up a rival kingdom to Angria called Gondal. The Gondal notebooks have disappeared. But we have the poems which Emily transcribed from them —poems in which she explored the passionate implications of the Gondal story. From these poems and a few other clues Miss Ratchford and later Miss Laura Hinkley in her *The Brontës: Charlotte and Emily* reconstructed the main lines of the Gondal epic and sought to establish its characters. This wonderful work of detection has made nonsense of many theories about the enigmatic Emily Brontë—the theory, for instance, that she had a lover; and the more specific theory that she was in love with her brother, Branwell: "Cold in the earth, and fifteen wild Decembers" we now know to be a lament uttered by a Gondal character, Rosina, for her long-dead husband, Julius. I suppose there is no home of genius haunted by the ghosts of so many deceased theories as Haworth Parsonage. It would be foolish, on the other hand, to suggest that the rediscovery of Angria and Gondal explains the whole Brontë enigma. "We take but three steps," said Keats, "from feathers to iron": but we need to take a good many more from that box of toy soldiers to *Jane Eyre* and *Wuthering Heights*. If it is absurd to suppose that a woman must have a lover in order to write passionate love-poems, it is no less crazy to assume that the Gondal poetry can be judged within the framework of the Gondal saga—that its terms of reference can be limited to Gondal's violent, Byronic characters and melodramatic plots, or to expect that the Gondal poems will be different in temper from those, ostensibly personal, poems which Emily transcribed into another notebook.

What we may confidently assert is, first, that the Gondal saga was a mere scaffolding, which, having enabled the construction of a number of poems, could then be dismantled and dismissed: Emily herself came to realize this; for, when she transcribed the Gondal poems, she paid no attention whatsoever to the order or context in which they had originally been written. And second, that the toy soldiers were only the efficient cause of this work—the trigger which fired it off: for the prime cause, we must look to Emily's nature and environment.

"My heart is but of fire and ice," runs the mediaeval carol. It might have been speaking for Emily Brontë, for her extraordinary mixture of passion and reserve, ruthlessness and tenderness. Miss Margaret Lane, in a recent biography, speaks of her "unsentimental harshness," of her "innocence," and again of her "melancholy, pessimistic, misanthropic, unsentimental, profoundly religious and independent nature." She was all that, indeed, but not all the time. Consider this passage from the birthday letter she wrote in 1845: "I am quite contented for myself: not as idle as formerly, altogether as hearty, and having learned to make the most of the present and long for the future with less fidgetiness that I cannot do all I wish; seldom or never troubled with nothing to do, and merely desiring that everybody could be as comfortable as myself and as undesponding, and then we should have a very tolerable world of it." That is the other Emily Brontë, of whom Mrs Gaskell wrote that "anyone passing by the kitchen-door, might have seen her studying German out of an open book, propped up before her, as she kneaded the dough." It is the note of commonsense, of down-to-earthness, which often accompanies—it did with William Blake—a certain kind of innocence and inspiration.

Innocence and inspiration are the keynote of Emily Brontë's best work. She was not an artist, in the sense of a writer preoccupied with problems of form, whose material is under control and who knows more or less what he is doing with it. Art for art's sake is the very last phrase one could apply to her work. What emerges from it—and most unequivocally from that great, mad poem in prose, *Wuthering Heights* — is passion for passion's sake, absolute passion. It is significant that Charlotte, her best critic, after discussing Emily's lack of worldly knowledge, lack of direct contact with people outside the charmed circle of Haworth Parsonage, should have written: "Her imagination, which was a spirit more sombre than sunny, more powerful that sportive, found in such traits ('those tragic and terrible traits of which, in listening to the secret annals of every rude vicinage, the memory is sometimes compelled to receive the impress') material whence it wrought creations like Heathcliff, like Earnshaw, like Catherine. *Having formed these beings she did not know what she had done.** If the auditor of her work . . . shuddered under the grinding influence of natures so relentless and implacable, of spirits so lost and fallen . . . Ellis Bell would wonder what was meant and suspect the complainant of affectation."

*My italics.

"She did not know what she had done." And, we may guess, she did not fully know how much of herself she had put into those "lost and fallen" spirits, Heathcliff and Catherine, or into the "relentless and implacable" heroine of Gondal, Augusta Geraldine Almeda. The germ of Heathcliff appears early in the Angrian saga—a small, black, foundling boy called Quashia, evil-tempered and rebellious, whom the Duke of Wellington brings up as his own son. But the full-blown Heathcliff has been nourished upon his author's secret life, on the marrow of her being. He, like Augusta of the Gondal poems, is an *âme damnée*.

There was a time, it seems, when Emily Brontë believed herself to be a damned soul, too. The Methodist upbringing she received from her aunt, her own reading of Cowper's poetry—both of these, perhaps, helped to persuade her into the conviction that she was a "destined wretch." In a poem written when she was still eighteen, she says,

> I am the only being whose doom
> No tongue would ask, no eye would mourn;
> I never caused a thought of gloom,
> A smile of joy, since I was born. . . .
>
> First melted off the hope of youth,
> Then fancy's rainbow fast withdrew,
> And then experience told me truth
> In mortal bosoms never grew.
>
> 'Twas grief enough to think mankind
> All hollow, servile, insincere—
> But worse to trust to my own mind
> And find the same corruption there.

The Calvinist sense of predestination recurs, seven years later, in one of the Gondal poems, "How few, of all the hearts that loved," with its Cowperish thought and tone; it is Augusta who is being addressed:

> O, fairly spread thy early sail,
> And fresh and pure and free
> Was the first impulse of the gale
> That urged life's wave for thee!
>
> Why did the pilot, too confiding,
> Dream o'er that Ocean's foam,
> And trust in Pleasure's careless guiding
> To bring his vessel home? . . .
>
> An anxious gazer from the shore,
> I marked the whitening wave,
> And wept above thy fate the more
> Because I could not save.

I should add, before leaving this, that Emily Brontë to a large extent grew out of this form of pessimism: she could say, later,

> But God is not like human-kind;
> Man cannot read the Almighty mind;
> Vengeance will never torture thee,
> Nor hunt thy soul eternally.

The struggle of the soul against a predestined doom is one form which the freedom motif takes in Emily Brontë's work. Another is the theme of exile. The Gondal poems are full of exiles and of prisoners; shutting out is equivalent, after all, to shutting in. And this theme, again, reached its peak in the outcast, Heathcliff. Its source, and the source of her obsession with the bitter internecine conflicts which racked Gondal, may well have been some split in her own personality.

Mr. Philip Henderson writes as follows:

Quite early, it would seem, she suffered from a desolating experience which left her with a sense of a life doomed and blasted at the outset. This gave rise to terrifying dreams and led to an idealization of childhood as a time of lost innocence . . . the poems suggest that it may have been an encounter with her shadow side or *animus*, later to be objectified in the demoniacal figure of Heathcliff. . . . At any rate, she was possessed with an elemental power which, in the silence and seclusion of her life, may very well have seemed to her to have had a separate existence. She was evidently familiar with the idea of the doppelgänger, that early nineteenth century formulation of the dual personality in which the conscious and unconscious minds pull in different directions.

However this may be, we are constantly coming across in the poems premonitions or echoes of the Heathcliff-Catherine situation. Mr. Lockwood's terrible dream is prefigured in

> The shattered glass let in the air,
> And with it came a wandering moan,
> A sound unutterably drear
> That made me shrink to be alone.
>
> One black yew-tree grew just below—
> I thought its boughs so sad might wail;
> Their ghostly fingers, flecked with snow,
> Rattled against an old vault's rail.

In F. de Samara's poem to Augusta, it could be Heathcliff himself speaking:

> And yet, for all her hate, each parting glance would tell
> A stronger passion breathed, burned in this last farewell.
> Unconquered in my soul the Tyrant rules me still—
> *Life* bows to my control, but *love* I cannot kill.

Heathcliff again in

> Shut from his Maker's smile
> The accursed man shall be:
> For mercy reigns a little while,
> But hate eternally.

And, to sum up this agony of mental conflict, this theme of a soul both divided against itself and desperately struggling against the limitations of life, let me set side by side a stanza from "My Comforter," and one of Catherine's speeches.

> So stood I, in Heaven's glorious sun
> And in the glare of Hell,
> My spirit drank a mingled tone
> Of seraph's song and demon's moan—
> What my soul bore my soul alone
> Within its self may tell.

What were the use of creation if I were entirely contained here? My great miseries in this world have been Heathcliff's miseries, and I watched and felt each from the beginning; my great thought in living is himself. If all else perished and *he* remained, I should still continue to be; and if all else remained, and he were annihilated, the universe would turn to a mighty stranger. . . .

And doesn't that remind us of a stanza from "No coward soul"?—

> Though earth and moon were gone,
> And suns and universes ceased to be,
> And thou wert left alone,
> Every Existence would exist in thee.

All this is the language of pure passion, transcendent passion. And Emily Brontë achieved it in *Wuthering Heights,* because Heathcliff and Catherine were, for her, much more than two passionate human beings: they represent the essential isolation of the soul, the agony of two souls—or rather, shall we say? two halves of a single soul—forever sundered and struggling to unite. So, as Charlotte said of *Wuthering Heights,* "every page is surcharged with a sort of moral electricity."

Charlotte goes on to say, "and the writer was uncon-

scious of all this—nothing could make her conscious of it."
It is true, I think, that Emily was a moralist on more than
one level. We can accept it that she was unconscious of
the full moral significance of *Wuthering Heights*—its
lurid and uncompromising antinomianism, in which
passion is substituted for grace as the justification for an
overriding of the moral law: it is difficult, indeed, to
imagine how the creator of Heathcliff and Catherine
could have consciously received the full charge of that
"moral electricity," and lived. But Emily dealt in other
levels of morality, too, where she certainly knew what she
was saying. She bears a strong affinity to Blake, in his belief that man-made laws warp and corrupt our natural
virtue, our original innocence. It was Emily Brontë, but
it might have been William Blake, who wrote:

> And what shall change that angel-brow,
> And quench that spirit's glorious glow?
> Relentless laws that disallow
> True virtue and true joy below.

And Emily could moralize on yet another level. We have
this picture of her, in adolescence: "Emily, half reclining
on a slab of stone, played like a young child with the
tadpoles in the water, making them swim about, and then
fell to moralizing on the strong and the weak, the brave
and the cowardly, as she chased them with her hand." I
would like you to notice those values: the strong and the
weak, the brave and the cowardly: they are extremely
revealing: they are a boy's values, rather than a girl's.

It has been remarked on that her kingdom of Gondal
was a more realistic and logical one than its rival, Angria.
This, no doubt, is why she seldom seems to have suffered
any revulsion from it, or felt any conflict between its
fantasy life and real life, as Charlotte did over Angria.
"Angria," says Miss Ratchford, "was a completely amoral

world where sin was shorn of its natural consequences, and such suffering as had to be admitted for romantic effect was an arbitrary visitation. . . . But in Emily's Gondal sin was real. . . . Emily admitted no arbitrary force for good or evil: her Gondals were free moral agents." And again, of these Gondals, Miss Ratchford says they were "a bold, hardy, elemental race to whom loyalty was the highest virtue and treachery the darkest crime; freedom was their dearest blessing and prison their deepest hell." Loyalty, treachery; freedom and its opposite: once more, a boy's values, a young man's values, not a girl's.

It is this third level of morality, according with the practical, sensible side of Emily Brontë, which gives an astringency to poems that might otherwise have been mere album verse: "Love and Friendship," for instance:

> Love is like the wild rose-briar,
> Friendship like the holly-tree—
> The holly is dark when the rose-briar blooms
> But which will bloom most constantly?
>
> The wild rose-briar is sweet in spring,
> Its summer blossoms scent the air;
> Yet wait till winter comes again
> And who will call the wild-briar fair?
>
> Then scorn the silly rose-wreath now
> And deck thee with the holly's sheen,
> That when December blights thy brow
> He still may leave thy garland green.

Even Emily's lighter verse is never frilly, or sickly, or trite. The exile theme, for example, which comes out in a group of personal poems written during 1838—poems written out of that homesickness which was so acute with her that, on two of the rare occasions she left home, she did actually begin to pine away—this exile theme never degenerates into an enervating nostalgia or a morbid self-pity.

Technically, her verse owes much to the logical side of her mind and to the 18th century style. Both these can be seen at work in her habit of antithesis, which has the effect of correcting any tendency in the poem to over-emotionalism:

> Shall earth no more inspire thee,
> Thou lonely dreamer, now?
> Since passion may not fire thee,
> Shall nature cease to bow?

Or this: the night wind is speaking:

> And when thy heart is laid at rest
> Beneath the church-yard stone
> I shall have time enough to mourn
> And thou to be alone.

Her occasional resemblances to Blake, on the other hand, cannot be attributed to literary influence. They are striking evidence of a certain mental affinity, a shared quality of innocence, childlike and visionary. I have quoted one passage earlier. Here are two more:

> And when heaven smiles with love and light,
> And earth looks back so dazzling bright—
> In such a scene, on such a night,
> Earth's children should not frown.

Or the second stanza of this:

> Child of Delight! with sunbright hair
> And seablue seadeep eyes;
> Spirit of Bliss, what brings thee here
> Beneath these sullen skies?
>
> Thou shouldest live in eternal spring
> Where endless day is never dim;
> Why, seraph, has thy erring wing
> Borne thee down to weep with him.

Emily Brontë was impatient, we feel, of the technique of verse. Her poetry is feminine in this, if in nothing else, that she cared far more about what she had to say than how she said it (I am aware, though, how risky such a generalization is). Her poetry is without frills—a poetry of direct, impassioned statement: similes are extremely rare; the vocabulary is small; the physical references limited to the landscape and weather of the Yorkshire moors, plus a few Gothic properties. Her metres are generally the four-square metres of the 18th century hymn-writers—another influence derived from her Evangelical upbringing. There is one rhythm, however, we should examine for a moment, since it was employed in three of her best known and greatest poems, as also in "Often rebuked, yet always back returning,"—a poem for which there is no MS. source, and which may have been written by Charlotte as an image of her sister. I say "rhythm," not "metre," because it has two metrical variants.

> Cold in the earth and the deep snow piled
> above thee!
> Far, far removed, cold in the dreary grave!
> Have I forgot, my Only Love, to love thee,
> Severed at last by Time's all-wearing wave.

The line here is basically a pentameter: but it is pulled out of the ordinary pentameter rhythm and given a different shape by three devices—by putting a stress on the first syllable of each line, by a marked caesura after the second foot, and by the use of feminine rhymes in lines one and three of each stanza. The effect of this rhythm I find extremely powerful, extremely appropriate. It is a dragging effect, as of feet moving in a funeral march; an *andante maestoso:* it is the *slowest* rhythm I know in English poetry, and the most sombre. The second variant of this rhythm we get in "The Visionary":

Silent is the House—all are laid asleep;
One, alone, looks out o'er the snow-wreaths deep;
Watching every cloud, dreading every breeze
That whirls the 'wildering drifts and bends the
    groaning trees.

Although this poem is based on a metre of six stresses to
the line, its rhythm has a family likeness to the pentameter
of "Cold in the earth." Again, a strong beat on the first
syllable of nearly every line, and a strong caesura—here,
after the third foot: the combination of the two setting up
a sort of counter-rhythm, four-beat working against the
basic six-beat "Sílent is the Hoúse—áll are laid asléep."
We get the same four-beat counter-rhythm in many of
the pentameter lines of the previous poem—"Cóld in the
eárth, and fífteen wild Decémbers." The effect is again
a dragging one; but it conveys a feeling of expectancy, of
time dragging for the one who watches and waits. And the
strong central caesura heightens this sense, as though the
watcher, breathless with expectation, had to draw breath
again in the middle of each line.

The same metre is employed in the greatest passage
of poetry Emily Brontë wrote, the stanzas from a Gondal
poem entitled "Julian M. and A. G. Rochelle (The
Prisoner)." Here, at the start, the tone is contemplative,
the lines are smoother, the six-stress metre is dominant:
but, at the fourth stanza, where the mystical experience is
mounting to its climax, where the soul is struggling to
throw off its fleshly chains and then being remorselessly
thrust back into them, the metre is roughened, the strong
central caesura reappears, and we receive the impression of
a labouring, gasping agony. The two lines which lead up
to this passage are: "A messenger of Hope comes every
night to me And offers, for short life, eternal liberty."

He comes with western winds, with evening's wandering airs,
With that clear dusk of heaven that brings the thickest stars;
Winds take a pensive tone and stars a tender fire
And visions rise and change which kill me with desire—

Desire for nothing known in my maturer years
When joy grew mad with awe at counting future tears;
When, if my spirit's sky was full of flashes warm,
I knew not whence they came, from sun or thunderstorm.

But first a hush of peace, a soundless calm descends;
The struggle of distress and fierce impatience ends;
Mute music soothes my breast, unuttered harmony
That I could never dream till earth was lost to me.

Then dawns the Invisible, the Unseen its truth reveals;
My outward sense is gone, my inward essence feels—
Its wings are almost free, its home, its harbour found;
Measuring the gulf it stoops and dares the final bound!

Oh dreadful is the check—intense the agony
When the ear begins to hear and the eye begins to see;
When the pulse begins to throb, the brain to think again;
The soul to feel the flesh and the flesh to feel the chain!

Yet I would lose no sting, would wish no torture less;
The more that anguish racks the earlier it will bless;
And robed in fires of Hell, or bright with heavenly shine
If it but herald Death, the vision is divine!

With that passage we return to the paramount theme
of freedom, and hear it in its most powerful variation, its
most absolute form. How far was Emily Brontë aware
of what she is saying here? One thing we can safely say—
she did not deliberately sit down to compose an image of
pure freedom. That is not the way poets work.

The passage occurs in a longish, not otherwise very
distinguished, semi-narrative poem about the discovery
by one Julian M., in a prison in his father's castle, of an

old childhood playmate, Rochelle. She is "pining there for Death to set her free": but it is Julian who frees her, hides her in his own apartments; and "By never-doubting love, unswerving constancy, Rochelle, I earned at last an equal love from thee." Now, one school of modern psychology, and the literary criticism that follows in its train, might interpret the poem as an image of the Death-Wish yielding to the power of human love. But nothing we know about Emily suggests that she was a victim of the Death-Wish, and the passage I have quoted conveys, not a yearning for oblivion, but something much more positive—a struggle towards a life, and a mode of being, beyond death.

What happened, I imagine, was that Emily Brontë sat down to write another poem about a Gondal episode, and half way through, the thing caught fire, took wing, and we get those stanzas which are barely relevant to the story of the poem, quite out of key with it, and whose intensity shows up the rest of the poem as superficial, insipid, unreal. Gondal, in fact, served two purposes. It touched off the fuse of Emily's imagination; and it enabled her to distance herself, so to speak, from the resulting explosion —to depersonalize the elements of thought and feeling which motivated her verse. We may describe Gondal as a set of moulds, made to receive her molten passion: after it had formed inside them, the moulds had done their job and could be discarded. Or we may put it another way— that Gondal was her attempt, though not a conscious one, to find what Mr. T. S. Eliot has called an "objective correlative." However we formulate the matter, we shall have to ask ourselves presently to what extent, as a set of moulds, as an objective correlative, Gondal was adequate.

Let us return for a moment to the stanzas I quoted. Do they reproduce an experience of Emily Brontë's? Our justification for conjecturing that they do has been well expressed by Margaret Lane: "There is a force and conviction about them, a ring of truth which makes it difficult to accept them as purely invented for one of the Gondal heroines; and the poem describes a spiritual adventure so rare that it seems unlikely to have been inspired by anything less vital than inner knowledge." Miss Lane is rightly suspicious of reading autobiography between the lines of poetry. But we must agree with her, too, that the "spiritual adventure" adumbrated in these stanzas does most remarkably correspond to all we can gather about the experience of the mystics. The brooding calm, the submissiveness, the mounting ecstasy, the sense of spiritual union with God—the Invisible, the Absolute; and then the agony when the trance thins away, "When the ear begins to hear and the eye begins to see; When the pulse begins to throb, the brain to think again; The soul to feel the flesh and the flesh to feel the chain":—all this follows and illuminates the pattern of mystical experience.

I think there can be little doubt that Emily Brontë at least came near enough to such an experience for her imagination to jump the gap. Her susceptibility to it would be rooted, perhaps, in her solitary disposition, her "refusal of ordinary life," the turning inwards of a supremely passionate nature. Such introversion is, no doubt, a neurotic tendency. But to label Emily Brontë as a neurotic, even as a neurotic of genius, is beside the point. The neurotic gives up the battle, flies the field—or rather, gets bogged down in it. Emily certainly escaped into Gondal: but she lived to fight again, to pursue her inveterate, one-man war with life's limitations, upholding her "banner with a strange device"—the device of freedom.

How did this solitary war ever begin? The environment of her childhood was not unhappy, not constricting. The Brontë children were allowed to run wild and to read what they liked; the little community at Haworth Parsonage was active, self-sufficient, bound together with ties of affection and respect. Though the countryside round it was bleak ("dreary" or "drear" are Emily's favourite poetic epithets), and the neighbours dour enough, the house itself was warm and elegant. And, as Charlotte wrote, "My sister Emily loved the moors. Flowers brighter than the rose bloomed in the blackest of the heath for her; out of a sullen hollow in a livid hill-side her mind could make an Eden. She found in the bleak solitude many and dear delights; and not the least and best loved was— liberty. Liberty was the breath of Emily's nostrils; without it, she perished." Even her fantasy world of Gondal reproduced, in colour and contour, the features of the world around her home: the "lone green lane," her escape route, only took her into a landscape as familiar as that of the Yorkshire moors:

> A little and a lone green lane,
> That opened on a common wide,
> A distant, dreamy, dim blue chain
> Of mountains circling every side—
>
> A heaven so clear, an earth so calm,
> So sweet, so soft, so hushed an air,
> And, deepening still the dream-like
>   charm,
> Wild moor-sheep feeding everywhere.

So why—we may be tempted to ask—why all the fuss? She wanted liberty. Well, didn't she have it? A reasonably satisfactory home-life, a most satisfactory dream-life— why, then, all this beating of wings? What was this cage, invisible to us, which she felt herself to be confined in? "In the midst of her life," wrote A. C. Benson, "which she loved in every smallest detail, she was haunted, it seems, by a sense of rebellion at her limitations." And of Heathcliff, into whom Emily Brontë, hardly knowing what she did, packed all the darker side of her nature, Miss Ratchford says, "Heathcliff's life went out, not of bodily illness, but of the constant beating of his spirit against the limitation of material existence."

My own belief is that the source of Emily Brontë's proud recalcitrance, her preoccupation with themes of captivity, exile and freedom, was her sex; the limitation of not being a man. "Stronger than a man, simpler than a child, her nature stood alone," said Charlotte. And then there is the testimony of M. Heger, whose school in Brussels the sisters both attended for a while. This is how Mrs. Gaskell gives it: "Emily had a head for logic, and a capability of argument unusual in a man, and rare indeed in a woman, according to M. Heger. Impairing the force of this gift, was a stubborn tenacity of will, which rendered her obtuse to all reasoning where her own wishes, or her own sense of right, was concerned. 'She should have been a man—a great navigator,' said M. Heger in speaking of her. 'Her power of reason would have deduced new spheres of discovery from the knowledge of the old; and her strong imperious will would never have been daunted by opposition or difficulty; never have given way but with life!' "

Add to this the values we have noticed earlier—her admiration for the strong, the brave, the hardy, the loyal; her condemnation of cowardice, treachery, weakness. Add to them Mrs. Gaskell's remark that "the helplessness of an animal was its passport to Charlotte's heart; the fierce, wild intractability of its nature was what often recommended it to Emily": and place beside this the extraordinary episode, related by the same writer, of Emily's mercilessly punishing her beloved and dangerous bulldog, Keeper, for a misdemeanour, with her own bare fists.

The sum of all these considerations is, surely, a masculine cast of mind in a woman's body.

Having said this, I must at once qualify it. There is no reason whatsoever to suppose that Emily Brontë *knew* what was the cause of her trouble, or consciously rebelled against being a woman. She projected her dissatisfaction onto the "real world" or sought compensation for it in her world of dreams. As she says in the poem "To Imagination":

> So hopeless is the world without
> The world within I doubly prize—
> Thy world where guile and hate and
>   doubt
> And cold suspicion never rise—
> Where thou and I and Liberty
> Hold undisputed sovereignty.

Mind you, she did not kid herself. Her strong—and, if I may so put it, masculine—rationality prevented any such self-deception. Later in the same poem she writes:

> Reason indeed may oft complain
> For Nature's sad reality
> And tell the suffering heart how vain
> Its cherished dreams must always be,
> And Truth may rudely trample down
> The flowers of Fancy newly blown.

Whatever else she may have been ignorant of, Emily Brontë knew the difference between the real world and the phantasy world. She says to Imagination, "I *trust not**
to thy phantom bliss"; nevertheless, "I welcome thee, benignant power." Similarly, she can in different moods

*My italics.

see death as an end or a beginning, a gateway to freedom
or an exclusion from it. On the one hand,

> "Well, there is rest there
> So fast come thy prophecy—
> The time when my sunny hair
> Shall with grass roots twinèd be."
>
> But cold, cold is that resting place,
> Shut out from Joy and Liberty. . . .

On the other hand,

> Thus truly when that breast is cold
> Thy prisoned soul shall rise,
> The dungeon mingle with the mould—
> The captive with the skies.

What is significant is that her passion, by which I
mean both the passionate intensity of her temperament
and her "ruling passion" for freedom, was orientated
always towards the inner world, not outwards—not even
outwards to the Nature which she loved. She makes the
point quite clearly herself in a stanza we have already
noticed:

> Shall Earth no more inspire thee,
> Thou lonely dreamer now?
> Since passion may not fire thee
> Shall Nature cease to bow?

This sharply-pointed contrast between passion and Nature
tells its own story. And it brings me to what must be a
fundamental criticism of Emily Brontë's poetry. By the
confining of her passion to the inner world—the world of
Gondal and of the "personal" poems; by her treatment of
Nature as a comforter rather than as a conduit through

which her passion could flow, or a field of symbols through which truth might be apprehended; by her uncompromising rejection of the world of men:—by all this, Emily Brontë's poetry was, we must say it, stunted of the full development which her genius might otherwise have attained.

Gondal satisfied her, on the whole. But Gondal, as a myth, was just not good enough to bring out her imagination at full stretch. This phantasy world, which she created partly as an escape from the real world, became a cage more confining than any prison cell of stone, and only in a few poems did she succeed in breaking free from it. Gondal was a solitary myth: but myths, to be poetically fruitful, must contain within themselves at least the seed of community. In Gondal's heroine, Augusta, that *femme fatale*—proud, ruthless, impatient, dominating, essentially destructive—bringing death to her husbands, lovers, children, a psychologist might well see an image of Emily's own conflict, the conflict of a woman who in phantasy imprisons or destroys men because she cannot be a man, who is blindly seeking thus to chain up or eliminate the man within herself. But Augusta, so far as we can reconstruct her from the poems, sets up no wider vibrations; she is insulated—the solitary heroine of a drama both too personal and too unreal to carry the universality of myth.

Charlotte Brontë's friend, Mary Taylor, on being told about the saga games of the Brontë children, made an exceedingly pertinent remark: "You are just like growing potatoes in a cellar," she said. Whether we take that "growing" as a transitive verb or an intransitive, the nail has been hit on the head. Potatoes, no doubt, could be made to grow in a cellar; but it is not the natural place for the process. Before she could write her mature novels, Charlotte had an extremely hard struggle—to transplant her potatoes from the cellar (from "the infernal world," "the world below," as she and Branwell called Angria) to the soil of the real world. Emily seldom made the attempt. She was a poet, of course; so you may say it was not necessary: and Gondal, at any rate in the moral and natural laws which governed it, was more like the real world than Angria. But it remains an artificial, a synthetic one, too remote from the fructifying influence of everyday concerns.

Had Emily Brontë been a dramatic poet, Gondal might have served to fulfil her potentialities. But her poetry shows little interest in character as such, or even in the moral conflict and the tragedy which issue from character or from the clash between freewill and necessity. Her early acceptance of predestination, though later it may have been discarded, profoundly influenced her work; and the idea of predestination cuts away the very ground from beneath drama. Her Gondal people, as we have seen, were vehicles for the elemental forces within herself; but the Gondal myth was not strong enough to discipline these forces.

In the same way, her Protestantism and furious individualism prevented her from becoming the great religious poet which otherwise she had it in her to be. Her God, like her Gondal, was too narrowly personal—a Being who, rather than reconciling her to humankind, justified her self-exclusion from it. And at times in her poetry we find this God confused, almost identified, with the "visitant of air" which inspired her verse and created Gondal; with the imagination:

> And am I wrong to worship where
> Faith cannot doubt, nor Hope despair,
> Since my own soul can grant my prayer?
> Speak, God of Visions, plead for me,
> And tell why I have chosen thee!

Even in the few directly religious poems she wrote, this
intransigent Protestant unorthodoxy is the keynote:

> O God within my breast,
> Almighty ever-present Deity!
> Life, that in me hast rest
> As I, undying Life, have power in thee!
>
> Vain are the thousand creeds
> That move men's hearts, unutterably vain;
> Worthless as withered weeds,
> Or idlest froth, amid the boundless main
>
> To waken doubt in one
> Holding so fast by thy infinity,
> So surely anchored on
> The steadfast rock of Immortality.

So it is, to return for the last time to our theme, that
the image of freedom in Emily Brontë's work, though
pervasive and ardent, seldom attains the full authority of
poetic truth. Too often we feel it as a kicking against the
pricks rather than as a free flight. Too often her vision
was fogged by phantasy. Whether we think of freedom
as the knowledge of necessity, or as the gift of a Supreme
Being in whose service is perfect freedom, it remains an
ideal which we can fully realize only through acceptance
of its limitations. Just as, in the world of men, freedom
without responsibility means anarchy or sheer madness,
so in the poetic world a passion for freedom will drain
away into phantasy unless it is directed by artistic
discipline. Emily Brontë did not, or not consistently
enough, impose such a discipline upon herself; and as for
the wider responsibility—she felt responsible to no one but
the God within her breast.

Yet, with these reservations, her poetry still has
tremendous force. There is a kind of poet who can only

hit the mark, so to say, by overshooting it, and Emily Brontë was one of this kind. The very exorbitance of her poems—a by-product, perhaps, of her Celtic ancestry— produces its own effect. She was, after all, an enthusiast.

> And truly like a god she seems:
> Some god of wild enthusiast's dreams.

What her poetry gives us, finally, is not an image of freedom but an image of man's inveterate, vain yearning for it; not the unbounded empyrean, but the beating wings. And she had the poet's right instinct for rooting her work in the most vulnerable, most wounded part of herself—in the deep cleft between the two opposed sides of her nature. It is this that I have tried to express in the last two stanzas of my own poem, "Emily Brontë":

> Is there one whom blizzards warm and rains
>   enkindle
> And the bitterest furnace could no more refine?
> Anywhere one too proud for consolation,
> Burning for pure freedom so that he will pine,
> Yes, to the grave without her? Let him mingle
> His barren dust with mine.
>
> But is there one who faithfully has planted
> His seed of light in the heart's deepest scar?
> When the night is darkest, when the wind is
>   keenest,
> He, he shall find upclimbing from afar
> Over his pain my chaste, my disenchanted
> And death-rebuking star.

II

GEORGE MEREDITH AND RESPONSIBILITY

"THOUGHT," said Pascal, "makes the whole dignity of man; therefore endeavour to think well—that is the only morality." It was the morality of George Meredith, and the basis of his philosophy. He described himself as "inveterate of brain." In *Modern Love,* his one great poem, where he dramatizes the problem of responsibility, the struggle for right thinking, in the context of the relationship between man and woman, we get this cry:

> Their sense is with their senses all mixed in,
> Destroyed by subtleties these women are!
> More brain, O Lord, more brain! . . .

The word, "brain," crops up all over his poetry. In the Lucifer sonnet he calls the stars "the brain of heaven." In "The Woods of Westermain," he writes of

> Pleasures that through blood run sane,
> Quickening spirit from the brain.
> Each of each in sequent birth,
> Blood and brain and spirit, three
> (Say the deepest gnomes of Earth)
> Join for true felicity.

That is the core of his philosophy: the idea that spirit is evolved from a happy marriage between man's reason and his blood—his animal force and instinct, with reason as the dominant partner. Over against this rationalist trinity

27

of blood, brain and spirit he sets Nature, the Earth, the Mother, through whom alone man may come to an understanding of himself. Wrong thinking cuts him off from Nature, and thus from the meaning of his own existence. As Meredith wrote of Shakespeare,

> But he can spy that little twist of brain
> Which moved some mighty leader of
>   the blind
> Unwitting 'twas the goad of personal pain,
> To view in curst eclipse our Mother's mind.

It is one of the extraordinary merits of *Modern Love* that, though produced, if ever a poem was, by "the goad of personal pain," though exploring the darkest corners of an unhappy human relationship, it never brings about that eclipse.

Meredith was an evolutionist, a believer in progress—not because he thought that any ideal of perfection can ever be attained, but because the struggle towards responsibility generates spirit. Man, he says, "Has half transferred the battle to his brain From bloody ground." And again,

> Contention is the vital force,
> Whence pluck they brain, her prize
>   of gifts,
> Sky of the senses! on which height,
> Not disconnected, yet released,
> They see how spirit comes to light. . . .

But Meredith does not value the animal and the rational elements in man solely for their contribution to the spiritual. He was, as G. M. Trevelyan said, "the poet of common sense," the poet of the golden mean—an all-round man who, in theory at any rate, stood for balance rather than eccentricity, and saw animal vitality both as a component of the good life and as a thing potentially good in itself. He is certainly no champion of asceticism: in *Diana of the Crossways* he wrote, "Nature will force her way, and if you stifle her by drowning, she comes up, not the fairest part of her uppermost!"

I have thought it necessary to begin with this cursory glance at Meredith's philosophy, partly because he was so much a poet—or rather, a versifier—of ideas, and partly because he was taken very seriously as a thinker, a sage, by many intelligent men of the two generations which succeeded his own.

Meredith's early work, the verse he wrote during the twelve years before *Modern Love* was composed, gives us no hint of anything more than a minor, and somewhat meretricious, talent. One excellent lyric, "Should thy love die"; the first, and very inferior, version of "Love in the Valley"; a few pleasant if insipid pastorals: apart from these, his early verse need not, and indeed could not, detain us for a moment. Its utterance is either bombastic or tinkling; its rhythms have the mechanical vivacity of a barrel-organ; its sentiment is often mawkish, sometimes maudlin. We never get the impression of an inexperienced but genuine poet casting about for his ordained themes—only one of dreadful facility. These poems are lush, superficial, diffuse, and bottomlessly uninteresting. Then we turn a page, and read the first poem of *Modern Love*:

> By this he knew she wept with waking eyes:
> That, at his hand's light quiver by her head,
> The strange low sobs that shook their common bed
> Were called into her with a sharp surprise,
> And strangled mute, like little gaping snakes,
> Dreadfully venomous to him. She lay
> Stone-still, and the long darkness flowed away

With muffled pulses. Then, as midnight makes
Her giant heart of Memory and Tears
Drink the pale drug of silence, and so beat
Sleep's heavy measure, they from head to feet
Were moveless, looking through their dead black
          years,
By vain regret scrawled over the blank wall.
Like sculptured effigies they might be seen
Upon their marriage-tomb, the sword between;
Each wishing for the sword that severs all.

It would be possible, no doubt, to fault that poem.
But we could not possibly call it superficial, or mawkish,
or facile, or uninteresting. The phrasing is strong and
sinuous; the language is in the grand manner, and the
combination of this manner with relentless psychological
realism produces an exceptional resonance of meaning.
The poem drops us right into the heart of a tragic
situation. A marriage has gone wrong: love has drained
away out of it, but the marriage-bond remains; and as
we shall see, this now lifeless bond is something far
tougher, far more galling than any chain of conventional
morality. What this poem adumbrates—and it is a major
theme of *Modern Love*—is the truth that a human
relationship, if it does not keep pace with the individual
changes and developments of its two participants, will
petrify. Meredith sums it up in the last poem of the
sequence:

Lovers beneath the singing sky of May,
They wandered once; clear as the dew on
          flowers:
But they fed not on the advancing hours:
Their hearts held cravings for the buried day.

The petrifaction of the marriage is hinted early—"She lay
Stone-still, and the long darkness flowed away"; and then,

seven lines later, this theme is clearly stated—"Like sculptured effigies they might be seen Upon their marriage-tomb, the sword between." How final that is, and how remorselessly the word "effigies" underlines the mockery which this marriage has become. But, though they are "Each wishing for the sword that severs all," the man and woman are not yet emotionally dead to each other: they are sentient, capable even of compunction. The wife's sobs, so "dreadfully venomous to him," are "strangled mute:" she is trying to spare him; and he, we soon discover, is trying to behave well towards her.

The surface plot of *Modern Love*, which is in form a sequence of fifty sixteen-line sonnets, may be outlined as follows. It is the story of a marriage which has failed, of the two partners' failure to find emotional release from each other, from the mortmain of their former love, in illicit relationships, and of their final reconciliation which also fails because it is but "a lifeless vow To rob a living passion." The situation is seen primarily through the eyes of the husband. But, through his sensibility and long experience of her, he is able, at times to enter into his wife's feelings and thus to suffer a double agony. In sonnets 1-19, we have the husband tortured by jealousy and by his hypersensitive response not only to the false artifice but also to the genuine appeal of a wife in whom there is still some "salt of righteous feeling": he tortures himself too, with memories of their happy past, and with the broodings of one who sits at the death-bed of a love that will not die. His anguish is intensified by his efforts to be both magnanimous and intellectually honest, and by the realization that nevertheless he is degenerating, disintegrating.

This deterioration takes shape in sonnets 20-39. The husband has approached another woman, with whom he finds an insecure, hectic kind of happiness, haunted by the shade of the old relationship—"A kiss is but a kiss now! and no wave Of a great flood that whirls me to the sea." His new love releases him a little from the emotional tie of the marriage: but it also releases a rush of cynicism about the relationship between man and woman, and spurts of cruelty towards his wife. As he had earlier anticipated, "In this unholy battle I grow base." The episode ends when, making love to "my lady," he sees his wife and her lover join hands. Jealousy floods back. He seeks a reconciliation. Husband and wife forgive each other, and try to resume their old life together. For a while there is peace, pity, affection, spiritual beauty even, in their relationship. But it is sterile, a dead end. Love cannot be renewed by an act of will or an aspiration of conscience. Pity, substituting for love, is in a sense the final betrayal, the worst falsehood.

> If I the death of love had deeply planned,
> I never could have made it half so sure,
> As by the unblest kisses which upbraid
> The full-waked sense; or failing that, degrade!

The wife, too, realizes their attempt is a failure. So, mistakenly thinking he still hankers after the other woman, she releases him and herself, takes poison.

Faced by a poem so different from the general run of Meredith's verse and so superior to it, we inevitably ask ourselves how it came about. Is it a novelette in verse, a tragedy of marital infidelity and its nemesis, conveying amongst other moral messages the poet's belief that there should not be one law for man and another for woman? Or, beneath the dramatic fictions of its plot, is there a deep layer of personal experience which should make us accept the poem equally as a study in morbid psychology? I have no doubt, myself, that *Modern Love* is the product of personal suffering, for which Meredith was impelled to choose a dramatic form so as in some degree to distance and externalize it. If we had no other proof of this, the internal evidence alone would be sufficient: we need only compare *Modern Love* with any of his other story-poems to feel an immediacy, a rawness, a self-exposure in the quality of the former, to be found nowhere else. Elsewhere we may be able to give intellectual assent. *Modern Love* compels the whole of us, mind and heart, to say, "Yes, this is true": and, after nearly a hundred years, its title still remains justified.

In 1849, at the age of 21, Meredith married Mary Nicolls. She was six and a half years older than he, daughter of Thomas Love Peacock, widow of a naval officer who was drowned before her eyes. She seems to have been very like the heroine of a Meredith novel—beautiful, witty, high-spirited, accomplished, a dashing horsewoman. She was also, we are told, "sentimental and sarcastic by turns . . . argumentative, and unacquiescent." She wrote poetry herself, too. An ideal mistress for a poet, we might think, but certainly not an ideal wife. Years after her death, Meredith said, "Peacock's wife became mad, and so there was a family taint." There can be little doubt that Mary was a neurotic; and when we turn to *Modern Love* we find a most penetrating definition of a neurotic intelligent woman: the wife there is described like this—"She sees through simulation to the bone: What's best in her impels her to the worst." In the same sonnet we get the lines, "Poor soul, if in those early days unkind Thy power to sting had been but power to grieve." Remembering Mary's barbed tongue, so free with the sarcasm and criticism to which her young husband was so abnormally sensitive, we may surely read autobiography here. Indeed, scattered all over the poem, there are passages where the acrid reek of misery is unmistakable—not the misery of the jealous, but that which comes from such a woman's instability and insensate demands.

Meredith himself was never an easy man to live with. He had a vulnerable sensibility and a bitterly wounding tongue: he was moody, proud, intransigent; and throughout his first marriage he had no success with his writing. The menage of this highly-strung couple was the worst possible for such temperaments—a "dreary sequence of duns, lodgings, dead babies and baffled literary ambitions." They were extremely poor; and their life had a curious rootlessness, less characteristic of the 1850's than of the intellectuals of our own time. Within these environmental conditions there was the increasing stress of the ordeal which is created by intense physical passion combined with mental and nervous exasperation: a woman who could be violent, derisive, exacting; a man, compelled to protect himself against the encroachments of her personality, and becoming in the process cold, brittle, pitiless, abnormally reticent.

By 1858, the estrangement was obvious. Later that year, leaving their one surviving child with her husband, Mary ran away to Capri with Henry Wallis, a painter. The next year, deserted by Wallis, she returned to England, sick and wretched. It is said that she wrote to Meredith in her extremity, imploring him to visit her, and that he refused. If this is true, we might well trace to it the passion of guilt and remorse which the husband feels at times in *Modern Love*. Mary Meredith died in 1861, and the next year *Modern Love* was published. On hearing of his wife's death, Meredith, who had been abroad, wrote to his friend, William Hardman—it is his sole recorded comment on her death—"When I entered the world again, I found that one had quitted it who bore my name: and this filled my mind with melancholy recollections which I rarely give way to." This tight-lipped and icy writing-off of his past tells us much about the man: but I think *Modern Love* tells us more.

We may now return to the poem, of which Mr. Siegfried Sassoon has so strangely written that "In *Modern Love* there is no revelation of the disharmony which caused this miserable break-up." Bearing in mind what we know of their temperaments and circumstances, consider this—one of the finest sonnets in the poem:

> Yet it was plain she struggled, and that salt
> Of righteous feeling made her pitiful.
> Poor twisting worm, so queenly beautiful!
> Where came the cleft between us? whose the
>   fault?
> My tears are on thee, that have rarely dropped
> As balm for any bitter wound of mine:
> My breast will open for thee at a sign!
> But, no: we are two reed-pipes, coarsely stopped:
> The God once filled them with his mellow
>   breath;
> And they were music till he flung them down,
> Used! used! Hear now the discord-loving clown
> Puff his gross spirit in them, worse than death!
> I do not know myself without thee more:
> In this unholy battle I grow base:
> If the same soul be under the same face,
> Speak, and a taste of that old time restore!

If this is not a "revelation of the disharmony" which caused the break-up of Meredith's marriage, I don't know what it is. They were "two reed-pipes, *coarsely stopped*" —ready instruments for the spirit of discord once the love-God had tired of playing upon them. And that question, "Where came the cleft between us? whose the fault?", for which answers are sought throughout the poem, together with the image of the two reed-pipes, does define the central theme of *Modern Love*—a theme fully stated in the famous lines,

> In tragic life, God wot,
> No villain need be! Passions spin the plot:
> We are betrayed by what is false within.

What *Modern Love* shows us is the demoralizing, paralyzing effect of a bond created, and then abandoned by love, as the two reed-pipes are played by the God, only to be flung aside. What it *tells* us is that man and woman are responsible for their relationship, that it should be an equal responsibility, and that, if it breaks down, the guilt must be equally shared.

It does not overtly tell us so. It is not a didactic poem, but a sequence of monologues, some dramatic, some lyrical, some satirical: in this respect it may remind us of Tennyson's *Maud*, another poem which the Victorians found deeply shocking. The surface plot of *Modern Love* is thin: its movement can best be traced as a series of impulses and revulsions proceeding from the conflict within the husband's mind, which swings wildly from jealousy to generosity, from pity to indignation, from hysterical egotism to a civilized sympathy, from regret to cynicism, from cursing to blessing. In doing so, the poem runs the whole gamut of thought and feeling which such a predicament as its hero's can provoke. Its dramatic shape, no less than its individual parts, is created by the straight conflict between instinct and intelligence, without the mediation of any accepted moral code.

We see this pattern of impulse and revulsion in the second sonnet:

> A star with lurid beams, she seemed to crown
> The pit of infamy: and then again
> He fainted on his vengefulness, and strove
> To ape the magnanimity of love,
> And smote himself, a shuddering heap of pain.

The husband, racked by jealousy, still has moments when he strives to be magnanimous. The effort recoils upon himself, in self-disgust and self-torture. But at least it is made—the effort to be civilized, to shoulder responsibility, to deal with the situation not in terms of prejudice or censoriousness, not by exercising the traditional rights of an outraged husband, but through intelligence and sympathy.

The subject of responsibility recurs throughout the poem, in several forms and at more than one level. There is, as we have seen, the idea that marriage involves equal moral responsibility and that if sexual lapses are to be forgiven in the man, they must also be forgiven in the woman. There is the idea, exemplified again and again in Meredith's novels, which G. M. Trevelyan defines like this: "God, as law, bids us observe that no action can fail of its consequences. Men can forgive each other, but deeds never forgive. The person whom you have wronged may pardon you, but the crime which he has pardoned will take some blind vengeance, either on you or on others."

Because *Modern Love* is a dramatic poem, faithfully following the moods of its central character, however discreditable some of them may be, we get different levels in the treatment of responsibility. The grandeur of "Passions spin the plot: We are betrayed by what is false within" becomes elsewhere the braggadocio and attitudinizing of

> I am not of those miserable males
> Who sniff at vice and, daring not to snap,
> Do therefore hope for heaven. I take the hap
> Of all my deeds . . .
> 　　　　　. . . That man I do suspect
> A coward, who would burden the poor deuce
> With what ensues from his own slipperiness.

That sonnet goes on with the husband finding in a drawer "a wanton-scented tress", relic of some old amour of his, and reminding himself—"If for those times I must ask charity Have I not any charity to give?" Three sonnets later, in contrast with the low tone and almost banal language of those two lines, we get a superbly heightened image of self-reproach and forgiveness:

> Come, Shame, burn to my soul! and Pride
>   and Pain—
> Foul demons that have tortured me, enchain!
> Out in the freezing darkness the lambs bleat,
> The small bird stiffens in the low starlight.
> I know not how, but shuddering as I slept,
> I dreamed a banished angel to me crept:
> My feet were nourished on her breasts all night.

That morbid last line ceases to be enigmatic when we collate with it two lines from another poem by Meredith: a Spanish girl says to her lord and master, "At my breasts I cool thy footsoles; Wine I pour, I dress thy meats." It is an image of utter humility and subjection; and there is no better instance of Meredith's psychological penetration and his honesty than that, after this impassioned outburst of shame and pity, the husband's dream of taking his wife back into his bed should be tainted by the attitude of the old Adam—of absolute lordship over the woman.

The efforts which the husband makes to behave well, to control with reason and sympathy his unregenerate instincts, bring their own reactions. What is the use, he grumbles at one point, of a man trying to be good and intelligent when the woman, with her romantic self-deception, her refusal to face awkward facts—and in particular the fact that a man must grow and expand—will not cooperate?—

> My crime is, that the puppet of a dream,
> I plotted to be worthy of the world.
> Oh, had I with my darling helped to mince
> The facts of life, you still had seen me go
> With hindward feather and with forward toe,
> Her much-adored delightful Fairy Prince!

The revulsion from the woman's tendency to retard and diminish a man, from the possessiveness which, as Meredith well knew, had been cultivated in woman by centuries of physical subjection or social inferiority, emerges again in sonnet XXXI:

> Some women like a young philosopher;
> Perchance because he is diminutive.
> For woman's manly god must not exceed
> Proportions of the natural nursing size.
> Great poets and great sages draw no prize
> With women: but the little lap-dog breed,
> Who can be hugged, or on a mantel-piece
> Perched up for adoration, these obtain
> Her homage. And of this we men are vain?
> Of this! 'Tis ordered for the world's increase!

Not only does the husband, in such passages of sarcastic petulance as these, react violently against the nature of women, and thus, indirectly, against his own better nature. He is also giving us a variation on another of the poem's themes—that a human relationship which remains static will become stagnant. If it is to devolop as it should, patience, forethought, imagination must be kept at work on it, civilizing the instincts, taming the ego. But there are times when the husband, despairing of the task, denies his saviour, rejects the intelligence.

> If any state be enviable on earth,
> 'Tis yon born idiot's, who, as days go by,
> Still rubs his hands before him, like a fly,
> In a queer sort of meditative mirth.

This, of course, is but a momentary and irrational revulsion. The supreme temptation to reject reason springs from reason itself. Meredith was painfully aware how dangerous it is for the partners in a married relationship to be analyzing it intellectually, constantly holding up to the light the fabric of their marriage, unpicking or patching it. He gives two hints of this at the end of the poem:

> Our inmost hearts had opened, each to each,
> We drank the pure daylight of honest speech.
> Alas, that was the fatal draught, I fear!

And again,

> Then each applied to each that fatal knife,
> Deep questioning, which probes to endless dole.

It is an irony to which *Modern Love* does full justice, that the exercise of intelligence, upon which an equal married relationship must depend, is also one of the forces most calculated to wreck it: partly because conscious analysis "that fatal knife, Deep questioning," cuts both ways and is a terribly risky instrument to use upon the living tissues of a relationship so deeply rooted in instinct; partly because women are in fact different from men, their reason still more subject to their emotions and likelier, therefore, to be frittered away in perverse subtlety. Moreover, the moral and psychological implications of the poem are drawn together in one final, apparently unresolvable, knot. If, in our search for the true meaning and practice of responsibility, we reject any specific code of sexual morals and try to replace it with some less rigid ideal fairer to the individual, we are thrown back each of us upon his own heart and mind. Strength of feeling is made the supreme sanction for a state of affairs it has already caused, and by which it is therefore compromised: the warring mind becomes sole judge over the conflict that divides it.

Modern Love, then, does not solve the problem it has stated. Poetry does not solve problems; it seldom even suggests solutions: what it does is to present problems in a form at once detached and more intimate than that achieved by any other mode of thinking: it enables us to see both the wood and the trees, and above all, through its habit of metaphor and image, to see them in a universal context of which we too are part. Poetry seeks always to relate, making more real for us, more full of meaning, the involvement of man with nature, of man with man, of thing with thing; and so it is the language of kinship. Since it is concerned to realize rather than to explain or judge, poetic thought is not invalidated by contradictions. "Do I contradict myself? Very well then, I contradict myself; I am large, I contain multitudes," said Walt Whitman. Now the thought of *Modern Love* embodies a contradiction, and leads us finally into a moral impasse. On the one hand, that kind of responsibility which we call marital fidelity is a good thing: on the other hand, it is good that we should be responsible, each of us, to the potential virtue, the developing selfhood in himself. When a married relationship has petrified, it obstructs this latter development: loyalty to the one will involve disloyalty to the other, and we must choose between the two conflicting responsibilities, since compromise is hardly possible.

But, *Modern Love* being a poem, we shall judge it by its measure of success in making us aware of the dilemma, not in solving the problem. Our criterion must be an aesthetic rather than a moral one. The fact, for instance, that Meredith proves himself way ahead of his time in his views about equality between the sexes, though interesting, is irrelevant. Now *Modern Love* is an uneven poem: between its peak passages there are troughs of very low pressure: and a number of the individual sonnets, even some of the best, are noticeably centrifugal —they seem to be moving compactly towards a certain point, but suddenly they fly off the handle, at a tangent. Well, you may say, this is justified because it represents the states of mind of the two chief dramatis personae: the husband and wife *are* distracted people, pulled this way and that by conflicting currents of emotion.

This argument would be more convincing if *Modern Love* had been written in dramatic form, either as a play, or as a monodrama, like Tennyson's *Maud*, whose variety of metres gave a more elastic medium for a wide variety of conflicting moods. But Meredith chose a form so similar to the sonnet's that he was committed to the concentration and the all-of-a-pieceness which the sonnet traditionally demands. This form does enable him to achieve at times an explosive intensity, as of a genie compressed into a small box. But, where his inspiration flagged or his taste lapsed, the form exposes it all the more mercilessly.

Again, the meditative sonnet-form is ill adapted to a dramatic cast of language—the hysterical ejaculations, the volte-faces, the satirical asides in which the husband indulges. And on the whole the best poems in the sequence are those where the dramatic element gives way to, or is no more than implicit in, a language of lyrical meditation. *Modern Love* has been severely criticized on the grounds of verbal garishness and of vulgarity in its sentiments. Meredith's taste, we must admit, was uncertain: passages like this cannot be defended:

> Devilish malignant witch! and oh, young beam
> Of heaven's circle-glory! Here thy shape
> To squeeze like an intoxicating grape—

Nor is it an adequate defence of the husband's occasional vulgarity, his cheap cynicism, tawdry attitudinizing, to say that cynicism and jealousy are vulgar states of mind but ones which such a man, overwrought, would naturally succumb to. If we argued thus, we should be confusing an aesthetic with a moral judgment. Poetry is all in the saying. We reject that stuff about the "intoxicating grape": we accept the terrible demoralization of those lines where the husband says to the other woman,

> A kiss is but a kiss now! and no wave
> Of a great flood that whirls me to the sea.
> But, as you will! we'll sit contentedly
> And eat our pot of honey on the grave.

I think it a defect of the form Meredith chose, that it does not accommodate, as a proper dramatic form might, some of its hero's more distraught and more unworthy responses to the situation. But we cannot put all the blame on the form. Meredith's language here is after the grand manner; and there is always a danger in applying the grand manner to a highly personal theme, that, if the poet's balance and impetus fail for a moment, the poem will drop into bathos or vulgarity. Meredith's style is not flexible enough to adapt itself to these sudden changes of mood and of emotional temperature: where a certain colloquial toughness is required, the language either remains high-falutin or becomes smart, flashy, flippant—one feels it condescending, as it were, in a hail-fellow-well-met way to the seamier side of the hero's nature. And there is one more point: Meredith, I am sure, was hampered by tabus of his time in respect of language. A poem at once so passionate and so realistic as *Modern Love* needs the verbal license of the Jacobean dramatists. "O bitter barren woman! What's the name? The name, the name, the new name thou hast won?" Webster or Tourneur would have rapped out the name, and half a dozen variants, with relish. Inhibitions of speech, in *Modern Love,* make the husband's jealousy a little less outrageous than it should be. We could bear to be shocked a bit more by the sexual implications of the poem.

The Victorians were shocked into fits, however. One might have thought that the most exigent moralist would be satisfied by *Modern Love*. Does it not tell us that the marriage-bond may not be broken with impunity, and that the wages of sin is death? But, although we may think Meredith was not outspoken enough, the reviewers in the intellectual weeklies considered him far too outspoken. "*Modern Love,*" said the *Athenaeum,* "contains passages of true beauty and feeling; but they are like the casual glimpses of a fair landscape in some noxious clime." The *Spectator* allowed Meredith no poetic talent at all—"a clever man, without literary genius, taste or judgment. . . . *Modern Love* (is) without any vestige of original thought or purpose which could excuse so unpleasant a subject . . . we can accuse it of nothing worse than meddling causelessly, and somewhat pruriently with a deep and painful subject, on which he has no convictions to express." The *Spectator* reviewer brings up the sound point, however, that "the form of the versification makes the smartness look still more vulgar." The *Saturday Review,* after a year of stunned silence—its notice did not appear till October, 1863—found its voice and declared the poem to be "an elaborate analysis of a loathsome series of phenomena which he is pleased to call 'modern love.'" The choice of subject, this reviewer affirms, was " a grave moral mistake. . . . So far from a condition of doubt and uncertainty on the general tone of matrimony being in any sense an interesting or attractive thing, it is one of the most disastrous calamities that can befall a nation."

That last sentence contains the real gravamen of the

charge against Meredith. His choice of subject affronted mid-Victorian society, which, intolerant as it was of sexual irregularity, had even less tolerance for the open discussion of it. In this society the marriage bond was sacrosanct; and a poem revealing the strength of the forces which may corrode this bond, exposing the love-hate element in sexual relationship, was a poem the Victorians could reasonably accuse of tending towards decadence. *Othello*, it is true, broached this same painful subject: but *Othello* was written by Shakespeare; and besides, it all happened long ago and in another country. But here was a young writer, with little or no reputation, venturing into these forbidden regions and daring to call his expedition *Modern Love!* Worse still, young Mr. Meredith seemed merely to dramatize his subject without taking sides: "I see no sin; the wrong is mixed." But Mr. Meredith should have seen the sin, however mixed the wrong may have been.

I have already done enough, I hope, to show that the critics were wrong in saying that Meredith had "no convictions to express." But the controversy between these critics, representing the great weight of public opinion, and the poets—Browning, Swinburne and Rossetti—who championed *Modern Love,* raises the problem of responsibility in quite another aspect. Wherever art and conduct have a common frontier, and at any period when art is taken seriously by large or influential sections of the people—when, therefore, it is likely to affect morality—the critic has a right to discuss (though not to confuse) both the aesthetic values and the social implications of a work of art under judgment. Obviously, in *Modern Love,* art and conduct have a common frontier. At any time the writer may feel the pull of two responsibilities—his obligation to set down clearly and forcefully the truth as he sees it, and his obligation, as a member of society, to further that society's moral and intellectual advance, or at least not to undermine its stability. From this apparent conflict stem certain absurdities we have seen in our own day—the absurdity of a humorless, wall-eyed censorship; and the absurdity of a starry-eyed but equally humorless romantic revolt against authority.

I say "apparent conflict" because I do not believe those two responsibilities are antagonistic except on the surface. The truths—or shall we say, the beliefs?—which form a culture, the thought-pattern of a society, have been built up, by trial and error, from a great number of individual enlightenments. Truth, in the last analysis, must be one and indivisible. There should not be one truth for the individual and another quite different truth for society. The poet's moments of vision contribute to the enlarging of the general imagination; and they may do so either by transfiguring the commonplace, glorifying the platitude, or by striking a light from their collision with accepted ideas and "normal" responses. Certainly Meredith, in running counter to the sexual morality of his day, could not have believed himself socially irresponsible; for, as we have seen, it was a central tenet of his that stability depends upon progress, whether in personal relationships or in a society as a whole. A sexual ethic denying woman the equal rights with man on which true love must be based, and hampering the development of her intelligence, so far from keeping society stable, tended always, he thought, towards social enfeeblement and disintegration. As he said in a letter to H. W. Strong, "Since I have begun to reflect, I have been oppressed by the injustice done to women, the restraint put upon their natural aptitudes and their faculties, *generally much to the degradation of the race.*"

If Meredith failed in responsibility, it was in responsibility towards his art. When we read through the mass of poems he wrote after *Modern Love,* we get the impression of a man from whom the blood has all run out. A great field of stubble they are—arid, prickly, dun; one harvest taken, and not another in sight. The "Lucifer" sonnet, the second version of "Love in the Valley," "A Ballad of Past Meridian," a few passages from "Ode to the Spirit of Earth in Autumn," from "Melampus" and "The Lark Ascending" — other than these, there is almost nothing we can honestly commend. What has happened to the poet of *Modern Love?* Consider the treatment in his later work of a favourite idea—the idea that wisdom only comes when it is too late, when the passion which needs it or could activate it has dwindled away. Now he writes,

> We spend our lives in learning pilotage,
> And grow good steersmen when the vessel's
>   crank!

or again, in "The Lark Ascending"

> Our wisdom speaks from failing blood,
> Our passion is too full in flood,
> We want the key of his wild note
> Of truthful in a tuneful throat,
> The song seraphically free
> Of taint of personality.

How pale and thin these lines are beside the great passage in sonnet IV of *Modern Love:*

> Cold as a mountain in its star-pitched tent,
> Stood high Philosophy, less friend than foe:
> Whom self-caged Passion, from its prison-bars,
> Is always watching with a wondering hate.
> Not till the fire is dying in the grate,
> Look we for any kinship with the stars.
> Oh, wisdom never comes when it is gold,
> And the great price we pay for it full worth:
> We have it only when we are half earth.
> Little avails that coinage to the old!

There, the idea has seeded deep in the heart of the
experience. We remember how young Meredith was when
he first married, how sorely he needed wisdom. But after
he had drawn up in *Modern Love* the disastrous balance-
sheet of that marriage, and locked it away for ever, cutting
his losses, it can be seen that poetic virtue has gone out of
him. For the rest of his life he is versifying ideas: his
poetry has become cerebral, laborious, over-stylized. We
get a constant compression of thought: metaphors pro-
liferate, struggle towards the light, choke one another in
a jungle of verbiage: the language is elliptic and self-
conscious, for ever taking short cuts or making elaborate
detours towards some pre-arranged idea, but more often
than not getting lost in the process—it is not so much an
exploration as a kind of steeple-chase. Compression of
thought there is indeed; but seldom does concentration
of poetic meaning result from it.

When we look at this later Meredith, we receive the
impression of a man writing against time, and writing
against the grain. Of course, he was for many years doing
too much: there were his novels and his journalism; he
was reading for a publisher; and reading aloud, for money,
to an old lady. Meredith's career is a dreadful example
of the way a writer's vocation can be tarnished by the
literary life. His poetry, after *Modern Love,* seems impatient, hurried, botched. And this is what I mean by
"failure in responsibility to his art." When the youthful
lyrical impulse has withered, a poet must attempt more
conscious investigation of experience: for this purpose he
may have to develop new techniques: but what he must
never do—and what, I think, Meredith did—is to lose
patience with the medium, to spur and whip words in
pursuit of ideas, to abandon that loving care for technique
which reflects the poet's perpetually-renewed self-dedica-
tion. Technique is not only the conscious ordering of

words and rhythms. It includes the discipline of creative
meditation, and the patience which will not broach
memories and ideas until they are matured. These, too,
are part of the *composing* of a poem: and where in
Meredith's later work can we find passages so composed—
or of such composure—as these from *Modern Love?*—

> Out in the yellow meadows where the bee
> Hums by us with the honey of the Spring,
> And showers of sweet notes from the larks on
>   wing
> Are dropping like a noon-dew, wander we.
> Or is it now? or was it then? for now,
> As then, the larks from running rings pour
>   showers:
> The golden foot of May is on the flowers,
> And friendly shadows dance upon her brow.

> We saw the swallows gathering in the sky,
> And in the osier isle we heard them noise.
> We had not to look back on summer joys,
> Or forward to a summer of bright dye.
> But in the largeness of the evening earth
> Our spirits grew as we went side by side.
> The hour became her husband and my bride.
> Love, that had robbed us so, thus blessed our
>   dearth!

The lingering sweetness, the golden undertone of
regret in such passages, Meredith never recaptured. Compare them with "A Faith on Trial," the poem he wrote
when his second wife died: it is long, garrulous, egotistical
—a rambling appeal to Nature for comfort and reassur-
ance: we should not call it insincere, but it is all somehow
beside the point and seems to expose the final sterility of
rationalism. Whether Meredith's philosophy of Nature
was in the end unsatisfactory to him, or whether it was
just that he failed to assimilate it thoroughly into his

verse, must remain a matter of conjecture. Certainly, both in his use of classical myth and in the symbolic material he invented, we are always made aware of some adventitious quality—a sort of intellectual opportunism which drags myth or symbol out of shape to fit his own brain-work. He has become a preacher. "A Ballad of Fair Ladies in Revolt," for example, merely preaches, with a great deal of perfunctory verbal decoration, the gospel of equality between the sexes which in *Modern Love* has been allowed to ferment beneath the surface and has worked itself into the very heart of the tragic situation. Or take "The Woods of Westermain." Here is a poem in which Meredith strove hard to unfold his philosophy—the right relationship between "blood, brain and spirit," and man's right relationship with his Mother Earth. But he has lost his touch. The central symbol, the woods of Westermain themselves, proves quite inadequate to sustain the complexity of his thought: he keeps on discarding it, then picking it up again and shaking it, like a man determined to make a mechanism work. But it won't work. It won't work, for all this violent effort of the will, because it is a prefabricated symbol, not an organic one growing out of the poet's experience. It remains an abstraction, without a heart.

And here, perhaps, we have reached the core of Meredith's failure as a poet, after *Modern Love*. He was a humanist who, because of his extreme sensitivity, tried to insulate himself from the human condition. Naturally, he did not put it to himself like this. He believed he was affirming civilization, forwarding the clearer apprehension of civilized values. And, no doubt, in his novels he was. As he wrote to his friend Maxse, "I strive by study of humanity to represent it: not its morbid action. I have a tendency to do that, which I repress: for in delineating it there is no gain. . . . Much of my strength lies in painting morbid emotion and exceptional positions; but my conscience will not let me so waste my time." Thank heavens, we may say, that when he wrote *Modern Love* he did not repress his strength for "painting morbid emotions." Suffering can purify, but it can also sterilize. The hideous and long-drawn suffering which produced *Modern Love* devastated him, I suggest, in two ways: it left a large area of scorched earth behind it; but also it forced Meredith to withdraw to a position in which he could never be so badly hurt again. In making this withdrawal, he cut away, surrendered, too much of himself: it was a major operation which left his poetry permanently invalid. Sonnet **XII** of *Modern Love* gives us these prophetic lines:—

> Methinks with all this loss I were content
> If the mad Past, on which my foot is based,
> Were firm, or might be blotted: but the whole
> Of life is mixed: the mocking Past will stay:
> And if I drink oblivion of a day,
> So shorten I the stature of my soul.

Meredith, I am compelled to believe, did drink that fatal draught. He tried to dissociate himself from his first marriage, to forget the agony of the past: and thus the stature of his soul, of his poetry, was shortened. In his later years, we are told, he had an almost pathological aversion from being given presents. This is surely revealing: for to accept presents means to accept relationship, responsibility; to be involved. And those long country walks he took—he could walk his friends off their feet, but perhaps he could never shake off the shadow of his own past. Reticent, proud, touchy, for all his vigour and intelligence he strikes us as the shell of a man, to whom nothing was ever quite so real again as that relationship with his first wife; a poet who could never again face such reality, and surrounded himself with abstractions, like a bodyguard, to keep it at a safe distance. Did he think he had given too much of himself away in *Modern Love?* If so, he never repeated the splendid mistake. Of one thing I am sure: the greatest tragedy of this tragic poem is that a poet lies in it, buried alive.

III

W. B. YEATS AND HUMAN DIGNITY

YEATS ENDED HIS POEM, "A Prayer for my Daughter," with this stanza:

> And may her bridegroom bring her to a
> house
> Where all's accustomed, ceremonious;
> For arrogance and hatred are the wares
> Peddled in the thoroughfares.
> How but in custom and in ceremony
> Are innocence and beauty born?
> Ceremony's a name for the rich horn,
> And custom for the spreading laurel tree.

And the poem which, in his *Collected Poems,* immediately precedes "A Prayer for my Daughter"—that great prophetic poem, "The Second Coming"—contains these lines:

> Things fall apart; the centre cannot hold;
> Mere anarchy is loosed upon the world,
> The blood-dimmed tide is loosed, and
> everywhere
> The ceremony of innocence is drowned;
> The best lack all conviction, while the worst
> Are full of passionate intensity.

These two passages summed up an ideal and a reality, as Yeats saw them. The good life is a settled way of life, rooted in tradition, flourishing in a courtesy simple and heroic. But this life is being swept away by a flood of vulgarity, of barbarism; and "the ceremony of innocence

53

is drowned." What men call "progress" today, Yeats saw
as the movement of a gyre, inevitable and retrogressive,
towards a new Dark Age.

What did he mean by "ceremony" and "innocence"?
Ceremony, to him, was the outward and visible form of
human dignity; innocence, its inward and spiritual grace.
When he speaks of innocence, he throws the net wide: it
includes integrity, spontaneity, the essential loneliness and
the potential self-sufficiency of the human spirit. Its adver-
sary is hatred, particularly "an intellectual hatred,"
which, in women especially, leads to a rabid and destructive opinionativeness. On the one hand

> Have I not seen the loveliest woman born
> Out of the mouth of Plenty's horn,
> Because of her opinionated mind
> Barter that horn and every good
> By quiet natures understood
> For an old bellows full of angry wind?

On the other hand

> Considering that, all hatred driven hence,
> The soul recovers radical innocence
> And learns at last that it is self-delighting,
> Self-appeasing, self-affrighting, ·
> And that its own sweet will is Heaven's
> will . . .

"Ceremony's a name for the rich horn"—the horn of
Plenty: a name, we might re-define it, for Yeats' idea of
true civilization. "How but in custom and in ceremony
Are innocence and beauty born?" That inward and
spiritual grace is born of the graces, the amenities, the
fruitful, sheltering and liberating tradition of a certain
settled way of life.

It is this tradition, and its bearing upon the concept of human dignity, which I wish to examine. Yeats was a poet—perhaps the last poet—in the aristocratic tradition.

> . . . When I was young
> I had not given a penny for a song
> Did not the poet sing it with such airs
> That one believed he had a sword upstairs.

The panache, the swagger of such lines is seldom far from the surface of Yeats' poetry. It derived from three sources —his childhood environment, the poetic movement of the Nineties with which his early work was associated, and a mettlesomeness and love of violence in his own nature. Let us consider the second of these first. Joseph Hone, in his biography of the poet, tells us how Yeats devoted himself to Lionel Johnson, "attracted by a certain stateliness of mind that seemed to be the counterpart of a little and beautifully formed body." The Rhymers' Club, which Yeats helped to found in 1891, and of which Johnson was a member, based its conception of life and letters considerably on the teaching of Johnson's master, Walter Pater. "Life should be a ritual," was one of their favourite sayings; and Edmund Dulac has written of "the world of aristocratic beings, cultured, refined, linked by a certain elegance of expression, a certain ritualism of dress and behaviour, that he [Yeats] had once realized about him, and always thought he might find again round the corner." Joseph Hone, again, speaks of "Yeats, with his almost Confucian sense of custom and ceremony."

Ritual, ceremony, stateliness—such words touch in the personality of Yeats himself and of his writing. Both in his earlier and his later styles, there is a stylishness—a conscious pride; a sense of the poet as a chosen being, an aristocrat in his own right, with a lofty mission. Not a mission to instruct, or to preach. The Nineties poets were in revolt against that Victorian notion — against, for example, in Yeats' own words, "descriptions of nature for the sake of nature, of the moral law for the sake of the moral law . . . and that brooding over scientific opinion that so often extinguished the central flame in Tennyson." These poets were profoundly influenced by the French symbolists, one of whom, Villiers de l'Isle Adam, endeared himself to the young Yeats by his remark, "As for living, our servants will do that for us." Yeats' bias towards aristocracy, like the French poet's, resulted sometimes in arrant snobbery: he could write, "Is not all charm inherited, whether of the intellect, of the manners, of the character, or of literature? A great lady is as simple as a great poet." In this formative period, then, Yeats was imbued with the idea of poetry as a religion in itself—the religion of art-for-art's-sake. Mr. Louis MacNeice has pointed out how "Yeats in his critical writings stresses the religious aspect of poetry but he tends to think of the poet as priest rather than saint. Poetry is a mystery cult, a ritual." And later, Mr. MacNeice makes a cogent criticism of Lionel Johnson's circle, which "seems to have ignored the fact that a ritual divorced from a belief—or from any belief except belief in a ritual—is vanity."

Yeats avoided this ultimate vanity, not by developing a religious belief, or even any political belief in the ordinary sense of the term, but through finding a subject —and an object—for poetry outside poetry itself:—"To write for my own race And the reality." Reality may seem a strange word in the mouth of a poet who engaged himself so pertinaciously in magic, astrology and the occult. But Edmund Wilson could say, "Yeats' sense of reality today is inferior to that of no man alive." And Mr. L. A. G. Strong's summing-up of Yeats' philosophy helps us to see past the apparent contradiction:—"Everything in nature

is a symbol, in the sense that it is an interpretation put by
our senses upon a reality we cannot otherwise know.
Belief therefore ceases to be a literal acceptance of the
evidence of the senses, or a criticism of experience for
apparent failure to conform to that evidence. It becomes
an intuition of harmony within a system." Yeats' recep-
tivity towards the supernatural, and his bias towards
aristocratic values, can both be traced back to his ancestry
and the boyhood years in Ireland. It was they which
inclined him to accept the anti-scientific, anti-rationalist
position of the Nineties' poets, and enabled him later to
build upon it a structure of poetry formidable in its
positiveness, its lack of compromise, its austere disdain for
sentimentality or rhetoric.

The Sligo where Yeats spent his boyhood holidays
presented an obstinately conservative way of life, the
peasants standing in a semi-feudal relationship to the
landowners. The latter were all Protestant, descended
mostly from Cromwellian soldiers or later invaders. His
own relatives — Pollexfens, Yeatses and Middletons —
formed a little patriarchal society, with the grandfather,
William Pollexfen, a ship-owner, at its head. William was
the stuff legends are made of. He had jumped off a ship
into the Bay of Biscay to retrieve an old hat. On another
occasion, as a passenger on a ship in distress, "judging from
some answer that the captain was demoralized, he took
over the command and, when the ship could not be saved,
got the crew and passengers into the boats." This was the
grandfather whom Yeats once saw "hunt a group of men
with a horse-whip." Then there were the uncles: one "was
a clever man and had designed the Sligo quays, but was
now going mad and inventing a vessel of war that could
not be sunk, his pamphlet explained, because of a hull of
solid wood." Another relative had designed a steamer:
"It had been built on the lake and dragged through the

town by many horses, stopping before the windows where my mother was learning her lessons, and plunging the whole school into candlelight for five days."

This society was not only violent and odd. It was also exclusive. Although its money had been made from shipping and milling, it maintained a strong contempt for trade: the Yeats branch of it, "having come down a little in the world," says Joseph Hone, "were all the more inclined to belittle people enriched by trade." Yeats himself rejoiced that he inherited "blood That has not passed through any huckster's loin." And, in his essay, "Poetry and Tradition," he said of the writer that "He has at all times the freedom of the well-bred, and being bred to the tact of words can take what theme he pleases, unlike the linen-drapers, who are rightly compelled to be very strict in their conversation." This snobbish exclusiveness shut out more things than trade. Both Nationalists and Catholics were despised: yet, though the Anglo-Irish gentry had no use for Nationalism, they had even less use for the English. They despised the English because they were always grumbling and kept no decent reticence about their private affairs. "My mother," Yeats wrote, "had shown them to me kissing at railway stations, and taught me to feel disgust at their lack of reserve."

Though its pride and sense of decorum excluded it from much, the Anglo-Irish gentry drew a compensating vitality from the peasants to whom it was attached in a free-and-easy relationship. Side by side with such men as William Pollexfen, who were becoming legends in their own lifetime and whom Yeats celebrated in the poems of his middle period, there were the sailors and the indigenous countryfolk. The sailors told him stories: the peasants offered the boy a wealth of Gaelic folk-lore and superstition. Banshees, fairies, ghosts, supernatural manifestations were as common, and as readily accepted, as blackberries—another order of reality, perhaps, but reality none the less: the seed of Yeats' later thought, which recognised no frontier between the real and the supra-normal, was sown here. The boy heard, too, about more unorthodox and officious spirits, such as the one which guarded a buried treasure and "looked like a flat-iron"— a manifestation only equalled when, years afterwards, Bernard Shaw appeared to the poet in a dream in the shape of a sewing-machine. The peasants and sailors, with whom Yeats spent so many of his boyhood hours, did more than fire his imagination; they provided more than the mere illusion of a vigorous, stable society: to the child of a family that had owned both land and ships, they represented the component parts of a community which was indeed settled, gracious and heroic in its simplicity—a community where a woman was remembered for her beauty, a man admired for his authority, his physical strength, his birth or his wildness, but where it was still impossible to buy for cash-down either respect or a post-humous reputation. "I am delighted," wrote Yeats, "with all that joins my life to those who had power in Ireland or with those anywhere that were good servants and poor bargainers."

Inspired by such a society, the young poet dreamed that "it might be possible to create an heroic and pas-sionate conception of life, worthy of the study of men elsewhere and at other times, and to make that conception the special dream of the Irish people." As he was to write in 1907, "Three types of men have made all beautiful things. Aristocracies have made beautiful manners, because their place in the world puts them above the fear of life, and the countrymen have made beautiful stories and beliefs, because they have nothing to lose and so do not fear, and the artists have made all the rest, because Providence has filled them with recklessness." His belief in this trinity of aristocrat, peasant and artist never faltered: at the close of his life, he put it into verse once again:

> Irish poets, learn your trade,
> Sing whatever is well made,
> Scorn the sort now growing up
> All out of shape from toe to top,
> Their unremembering hearts and
>   heads
> Base-born products of base beds.
> Sing the peasantry, and then
> Hard-riding country gentlemen,
> The holiness of monks, and after
> Porter-drinkers' randy laughter;
> Sing the lords and ladies gay
> That were beaten into the clay
> Through seven heroic centuries;
> Cast your mind on other days
> That we in coming days may be
> Still the indomitable Irishry.

Two of the writers Yeats had most admired are echoed there. The harking-back to a simple, gay, heroic society reminds us of the mediaevalism of William Morris, who was Yeats' strongest early influence. The attack on the Common Man is in the slashing, reckless style of Swift. The Common Man, says Yeats, "the sort now growing up," is "all out of shape"—ugly and without elegance: he is "unremembering"—he has no past, no tradition. This point of view, in its relevance or lack of relevance to our present day, we must examine later. But I should point out here that its source was in the society which shaped Yeats' boyhood. The little world of Sligo was a world (I quote Sir Maurice Bowra) where "personality was still as important as it had been in the eighteenth century, and a man was entitled to be unlike his fellows." The "Century of the Common Man," on the other hand—and it is, perhaps, one of our least admirable characteristics—does not, for all the lip-service we in the West pay to the importance of the individual, encourage a man to be unlike his fellows.

Mind you, Yeats' picture of an aristocratic golden age was, partly at least, a fake. When he returned to Ireland in 1896, and first met Lady Gregory, with whom he was to found the Abbey Theatre, he had little acquaintance with the aristocracy. Because her house, Coole Park, offered him an elegant and cultured life, he generalized from it, persuading himself that it was a type of the Big House, and Lady Gregory typical of the big Irish landowner, ignoring the fact—as Mr. MacNeice tartly but truly puts it, "that in most cases these houses maintained no culture worth speaking of—nothing but an obsolete bravado, an insidious bonhomie and a way with horses." Yeats admired Lady Gregory because her "point of view was founded, not on narrow modern habit, but upon her sense of great literature, upon her own strange feudal, almost mediaeval youth." Back to William Morris again: but, Yeats believed, with a difference: "Ruskin and Morris had spent themselves in vain because they had found no passion to harness to their thought, but here were un-wasted passion and precedents in the popular memory for every needed thought and action." "Here" was, of course, Ireland. And Ireland did turn Yeats into a great poet, though not altogether in the ways he had expected.

Let me now sum up the several qualities which Yeats believed he found in the aristocratic tradition. I will then try to show you how they worked out in the practice of his poetry, and how far they may still be relevant to our contemporary thinking about human dignity and human selfhood. We have seen, first, the emphasis which Yeats laid upon custom and ceremony, upon a conservative pattern of life exemplified for him by the relationship between land-owner and peasant, and in the specific virtues of each class. This is akin to the 18th century idea of a settled hierarchy both in social relations and in the whole order of the universe. He believed that Ireland, where the Anglo-Irish Ascendancy still kept alive the Augustan tradition, offered such a pattern of life, and that her people had reserves of "unwasted passion" which the poet could harness to his work: but, so he said, the "popular poets have not touched her heart; her poetry when it comes will be distinguished and lonely." Second, Yeats saw the common factor in aristocrat, peasant and artist as a lack of fear: all three create beautiful things because, for different reasons, they are above fear or beyond it—above, that is to say, the bourgeois preoccupation with material advantage, with "getting on." It was a precept of Confucius, that a gentleman never competes. Yeats' father, who so greatly influenced his thought, used to say, "A gentleman is such simply because he has not the doctrine of *getting on* and the habit of it." Yeats often opposes to the anxiety of the modern, middle-class, progressive world the "gaiety" which springs from an order of hereditary or natural aristocrats. Third, the continuity and respect for personality implicit in the aristocratic tradition gives the poet scope for ancestor-worship and for hero-worship: Yeats' own poetry testifies to this: the Irish patriots; the great Anglo-Irish figures — Burke, Grattan, Berkeley, Swift; his own relatives and friends—all move and have their being in the same legendary milieu as the gods and heroes of Celtic myth. Finally, the pride, the confidence, the insouciance of the aristocratic tradition communicated themselves to Yeats' style, so that his verse conferred dignity upon any subject it touched.

Let us consider this last point first; for the proof of the pudding is in the eating, and it will be impossible to dismiss the aristocratic tradition as a fantasy or an anachronism if we do indeed find it flavouring and strengthening the poet's work. Yeats wrote, "In life courtesy and self-possession, and in the arts style, are the sensible impressions of the free mind, for both arise out of a deliberate shaping of all things, and from never being swept away, whatever the emotion, into confusion or dulness." How clearly those last phrases echo the Augustan attitude! He wrote them in 1907, when he was emerging from the Celtic twilight and stood on the watershed between his early and his later style. Three years before, he had published *In The Seven Woods*, which was still very much after the Ninety-ish manner. Three years later, in 1910, *The Green Helmet* appeared, its poems giving us a new kind of utterance—a grand manner still, but purged, unequivocal; the language brilliant and firm where it had been misty and wavering. From now on, though some of his poems are extremely difficult—largely because of their esoteric symbolism—they follow the tendency referred to by Yeats in a letter of 1926 to Professor Grierson:—"My own verse has more and more adopted—seemingly without any will of mine—the syntax and vocabulary of common speech." Mr. Louis MacNeice has some useful comments on this point:—"In diction, and in syntax also, Yeats offered us a compromise with the Wordsworthian 'real language of men.' Wordsworth set out to use the words of common speech, though, as Coleridge pointed out, in theory he meant to exclude the common speech of the educated classes. Yeats took the words of common speech, including those of the educated, but he put a twist on them; as A. E. says, he *made them aristocratic."* And Edmund Wilson, writing of the period inaugurated by *The Green Helmet,* says, "Yeats inhabits, in this phase, a world of pure intense emotions expressed in distinct fine images. His words, no matter how prosaic, are always somehow luminous and noble. . . . He finds his subjects

now in the events of his own life, no longer transposed
into romantic convention, and in the public affairs of
Ireland. And he succeeds in dignifying such subjects, as
perhaps no other contemporary poet has done, at the same
time that he never ceases to deal with them without
sentimentality and in the plainest language."

The operative word is "dignifying." At one end of the
scale, Yeats' verse could give dignity to topical and
parochial events—the rows at the Abbey Theatre, the
squabble over Hugh Lane's pictures. At the other end, he
could magnify what was already of heroic proportions.
Maud Gonne, for example, to whom his greatest love
poems were addressed, and of whom he wrote "she looked
as though she lived in an ancient civilization where all
superiorities, whether of the mind or the body, were a part
of public ceremonial." This tall, beautiful, statuesque
creature, already—so to speak—more than life-size, he
transforms into a legendary woman, a Helen.

> Why should I blame her that she filled my days
> With misery, or that she would of late
> Have taught to ignorant men most violent ways,
> Or hurled the little streets upon the great,
> Had they but courage equal to desire?
> What could have made her peaceful with a mind
> That nobleness made simple as a fire,
> With beauty, like a tightened bow, a kind
> That is not natural in an age like this,
> Being high and solitary and most stern?
> Why, what could she have done, being what she is?
> Was there another Troy for her to burn?

That poem from the 1910 volume gives us the feel of
Yeats' second manner and epitomises the aristocratic bias
in his thought. Except for the line "Being high and solitary
and most stern," there is not a trace of his Ninety-ish style.
The vocabulary is plain, unshowy: writing of dramatic

poetry, he said "certain words must be dull and numb," and we can see here how successfully this theory was applied at times to the lyric also. Again, Yeats had an exceptionally fine ear for rhythm: he was a master in the art of playing off colloquial rhythms against the basic metre: the penultimate line, with its inversion of stresses, is a fine example of this—"why, what coúld she have dóne, béing what she ís?" This line gathers the thought up and drives it at the epigrammatic conclusion, "Was there another Troy for her to burn?" The thought is typical—scorn for the rabble, admiration for the heroic leader, who would hurl the little streets upon the great. There is no paradox about this, or at least Yeats felt none: ignorant men, who have not "courage equal to desire," are no less contemptible because they happen to be led by a heroine: a heroine is no less a heroine because the metal she works in is base. And this heroine, Maud Gonne—what Yeats admires in her most is not her patriotism, not even her beauty and nobleness, but the way she accepts and fulfils the necessity of her nature.

"Why should I blame her," he says of the woman whom so long and despairingly he loved. Here is another façet of the aristocratic ideal—magnanimity. We have it again in a poem from his next volume:

> And what of her that took
> All till my youth was gone
> With scarce a pitying look?
> How could I praise that one?
> When day begins to break
> I count my good and bad,
> Being wakeful for her sake,
> Remembering what she had,
> What eagle look still shows,
> While up from my heart's root
> So great a sweetness flows
> I shake from head to foot.

Those last three lines give us an image of magnanimity; not the kind which makes a conscientious effort to forgive a wrong and rise above it, but pure, unforced magnanimity. They express the poet's recognition of a love which, though in one sense it was fruitless, distilled a miraculous flow of sap and sweetness. Now to be able to write thus about a woman who, if I may put it vulgarly, has kept on turning you down, needs a kind of magnanimity which cannot be acquired by frequenting the psychoanalysts. It consists, not in detachment or self-knowledge, but in having committed yourself to love, absolutely and innocently.

You may say those lines are just a magnificent gesture: yes, but such gestures can only proceed from an heroic view of life. Yeats' view was the heroic one, not the tragic. Hence we get, in the passage I have quoted, that note of exhilaration which I referred to earlier as "gaiety." We hear it again and again: in the refrain to "His Phoenix"—"I knew a phoenix in my youth, so let them have their day": or in "Lapis Lazuli":

> All perform their tragic play,
> There struts Hamlet, there is Lear,
> That's Ophelia, that Cordelia;
> Yet they, should the last scene be there,
> The great stage curtain about to drop,
> If worthy their prominent part in the play,
> Do not break up their lines to weep.
> They know that Hamlet and Lear are gay;
> Gaiety transfiguring all that dread.

Gaiety, one could almost say, is for Yeats the mode of magnanimity—part, certainly, of that "heroic and passionate conception of life" through which he transformed a beautiful but often tiresome revolutionary into "a woman Homer sung." Heroic and Homeric again, an image of the innocent soul which "learns at last that it is self-delighting," are these lines from "An Irish Airman Foresees His Death":

> Nor law, nor duty bade me fight,
> Nor public men, nor cheering crowds,
> A lonely impulse of delight
> Drove to this tumult in the clouds.

It would be a great mistake, however, to carry this heroic context too far, or to equate the heroic with the aristocratic. Although, as a boy, Yeats had perhaps enough passion, imagination and capacity for hero-worship to have made an epic poet in a different age within such a community as Sligo gave him, history and his own divided, introspective nature would in any case have stopped him from developing on these lines. Instead, he grew sophisticated, critical, impatient, as any man may to whom his times do not seem to offer a subject that fits his talent. The impact of this sophistication upon his aristocratic tradition and the images of his youngest days is the key to a great deal in his poetry. It is, for one thing, the key to his particular kind of romanticism; for romanticism is what happens when the heroic begins to doubt itself: it is the heroic betraying its own loss of innocence by protesting too much. There is, in much of the poetry of Yeats' middle period, the air of a last-ditch fight—"We were the last romantics—chose for theme Traditional sanctity and loveliness."

Yeats' earlier poetry demonstrates this lack of conviction, in the plangent rhythms and twilight colouring which reveal the nostalgia of the exile. Here he is embroidering upon the Celtic gods and heroes; not realizing a myth, or adapting it to a modern context; not, except in *The Countess Kathleen*, crystallizing a moral subject. "I made my song a coat Covered with embroideries Out of old mythologies." When he wrote that, Yeats had begun to play down the Celtic mythology, and use the other side of his tradition—the ancestral figures of his childhood, and there was no longer any lack of conviction.

> Beyond that ridge lived Mrs. French, and
> once
> When every silver candlestick or sconce
> Lit up the dark mahogany and the wine,
> A serving man that could divine
> That most respected lady's every wish
> Ran and with the garden shears
> Clipped an insolent farmer's ears
> And brought them in a little covered dish.

Of this respected lady, "gifted with so fine an ear," as of other characters in the later poems, we may say that she is all very fine, but she is no longer a purely heroic figure. Passion has left them a little, and irony crept in to make up the deficit. There is an air about them—as about certain noblemen and officials in Tchehov—of faint distortion, of imposed eccentricity or conscious under-emphasis.

Anglo-Irish society *was* falling into the same sort of decadence then as had fallen the society about which Tchehov wrote. And the native Irish?—"Romantic Ireland's dead and gone, It's with O'Leary in the grave." So, at least, Yeats thought, till the Easter Rebellion. His admiration for O'Leary was significant. The moral fastidiousness of this great old Irish patriot, who could say "There are things a man must not do to save a nation," appealed to the aristocratic fastidiousness in Yeats. The Easter Rebellion of 1916 caused Yeats to change his tune. It was a gesture after his heart, in the grand old romantic manner: amongst its leaders were poets and scholars, his own friends: and it had that appeal which action and violence always had for Yeats, when they arose from an exorbitant inner necessity, from passion.

> And what if excess of love
> Bewildered them till they died?
> I write it out in a verse—
> MacDonagh and MacBride
> And Connolly and Pearse
> Now and in time to be,
> Wherever green is worn,
> Are changed, changed utterly:
> A terrible beauty is born.

But "Easter 1916" is the great poem it is because it is not a simply assenting poem. It has a tension, set up by the conflict between hero-worship and scepticism, and for this reason is a truly modern poem. Yeats can admire the bravery and devotion of the rebel leaders; but at the same time he can criticize Maud Gonne, because her mind had become "a bitter, an abstract thing"; and even while praising the hero, he deplores the fanatic—"Too long a sacrifice Can make a stone of the heart."

The wars that followed in Ireland were a different proposition. They lacked the glamour of romantic gestures and heroic failures. The whole country being involved now, the artist could no longer occupy a ringside seat: the widening split between Anglo-Irish gentry and the Irish people could no longer be bridged by "custom and ceremony." For Yeats, this seemed the beginning of a cycle when "The best lack all conviction, while the worst Are full of passionate intensity." One part of his mind could envy the men of action: the other part must turn away—"turn towards my chamber, caught In the cold snows of a dream,"—and meditate upon the apparent powerlessness of idealism before brute reality:

> The night can sweat with terror as before
> We pieced our thoughts into philosophy,
> And planned to bring the world under a rule,
> Who are but weasels fighting in a hole.

or,

> O but we dreamed to mend
> Whatever mischief seemed
> To afflict mankind, but now
> That winds of winter blow
> Learn that we were crack-pated
> when we dreamed.

But the aristocratic tradition, which had led him to this impasse, nevertheless, because it presumes responsibility, prevented Yeats' detachment becoming mere escape. The various public controversies in which he had engaged, his work in the Irish Senate later, are sufficient to show his sense of responsibility. Yet he is, throughout, the autocrat who feels a passionate love for the Cause but also a certain impatience and contempt for the human instruments with which he has to work. Sooner or later there always recurred the mood of "The seeming needs of my fool-driven land." No doubt, he went into politics as he explored the occult, not least for what they could give to his poetry. But he believed, also, that he had something to give in return—something more than the hard-headed, business-like Yeats who had made a success of the Abbey Theatre. This other contribution to politics, a theoretical one, is sufficiently indicated in a speech he made during the Tailteann Games of 1924:—"The world," he said, "can never be the same. The stream has turned backwards, and generations to come will have for their task, not the widening of liberty, but recovery from its errors—the building up of authority, the restoration of discipline, the discovery of a life sufficiently heroic to live without the opium dream."

This was all very shocking—a plea for something like totalitarianism at a time when Hitler and Mussolini were only names to most of us. And nine years later, when Yeats began to flirt with General O'Duffy's Blueshirt movement, he could be safely branded as a Fascist. Not that he cared: Yeats had a pugnacious element, and enjoyed trailing his coat. Not that he had any illusions about the Blueshirt movement: as he wrote to a friend, "Doubtless I shall hate it (though not so much as I hate Irish democracy)." It was all very shocking, perhaps, but it should not have been so surprising; Yeats had been saying that sort of thing in his poetry for the last twenty years: he believed that the aristocratic tradition could best be carried on, *faute de mieux*, by a Fascist movement. "He was disappointed and was also surprised," Mr Hone tells us, "—it is a proof of the credulity which was often observed in him—when politics went on very much as before, the Blueshirts as demagogic as the rest." So he severed his connection with the movement. But he did not, otherwise, change his mind: he had for years been exercised as to the best method for adapting the aristocratic, Protestant tradition of the Anglo-Irish to Gaelic nationalism: he continued in his verse to attack his own—not altogether historical—conception of "Whiggery."

> Whether they knew or not
> Goldsmith and Burke, Swift and the Bishop
> of Cloyne
> All hated Whiggery; but what is Whiggery?
> A levelling, rancorous, rational sort of mind
> That never looked out of the eye of a saint
> Or out of drunkard's eye.

So there we have it again—the anti-equalitarian, anti-rationalist feeling which informed Yeats' work throughout. A man of versatile mind and powerful intellectual curiosity, he nevertheless distrusted the rule of reason. In "A Prayer for Old Age," he wrote

> God guard me from those thoughts men think
> In the mind alone;
> He that sings a lasting song
> Thinks in a marrow-bone;

This is quite different from D. H. Lawrence's cult of the blood, the dark centres. It is a warning against shallow intellectualism, against thought which is not rooted deep in a man and thus cannot represent or satisfy the whole man. Yeats' poetic ideal was to combine passion with precision, and to pursue that innocence which, I have suggested, includes both spontaneity and integrity: his poetic achievement was the extent to which his verse conveys the whole man. He was tirelessly engaged in the search for identity. So far from being silenced by old age, he turned upon it with the eager ferocity of genius and made it yield up its meaning to him:

> Consume my heart away: sick with desire
> And fastened to a dying animal
> It knows not what it is.

Side by side with the search for identity—for the essential self, the marrow in the bone—ran the search for imaginative enlargement. Here, to aid him, Yeats called upon the doctrine of the Anti-Self, which he sums up in "Ego Dominus Tuus":

> By the help of an image
> I call to my own opposite, summon all
> That I have handled least, least looked upon.

All along the line, Yeats' poetry was quickened by the clash of opposites: the self and the anti-self; the conflict within himself between realism and mysticism, the practical, responsible man and the inspired fool; between the patriot and the artist, the sceptic and the romantic: and we may fairly say that the personality of his verse is created by that uneasy alliance, which we noted in "a Prayer for My Daughter," between spiritual anarchism and a kind of temporal good form. What Paul Valéry called "la sainte impatience"—divine discontent—never died in Yeats.

> Infirm and aged I might stay
> In some good company,
> I who have always hated work,
> Smiling at the sea,
> Or demonstrate in my own life
> What Robert Browning meant
> By an old hunter talking with Gods;
> But I am not content.

He is an actor, who must extract the last ounce from each successive rôle he is called to play—"Grant me an old man's frenzy, Myself must I remake Till I am Timon and Lear.". . .

Well then, how far can we accept this great composite picture of human dignity which Yeats' poetry offers us? Is the aristocratic tradition dead? or, if not dead, is it worth reviving? I think the answer depends finally upon the measure of assent we can give to the ideas of hero-worship and ancestor-worship. In *The Countess Kathleen*, you remember, the angel says "The Light of Lights Looks always on the motive, not the deed." Unfortunately, this is also what the psychoanalysts look on; and we have paid for Freud's great contribution to human knowledge by yielding up much of our belief in the great man, the exceptional man. In a deterministic world, its human element interpreted by a deterministic psychology, what place is there for the hero? And in an age whose most powerful figures have been Lenin, Hitler and Stalin, can we afford the "great man"?

Such questions Yeats answered, or brushed aside, in a characteristic way. "We"—he is writing of the Irish—"are certain that nothing can give dignity to human nature but the character and energy of its expression. We do not even ask that it shall have dignity so long as it can burn away all that is not itself." Yeats, in fact, is looking upon neither the motive nor the deed separately, but on deed and motive together as and when they represent the essential man and therefore the whole man. Is not this behind what he is saying, in the last stanza of "A Dialogue of Self and Soul," with its gaiety, its belief that the soul may recover "radical innocence," and in so doing learn "that its own sweet will is Heaven's will,"?

> I am content to follow to its source
> Every event in action or in thought;
> Measure the lot; forgive myself the lot!
> When such as I cast out remorse
> So great a sweetness flows into the breast
> We must laugh and we must sing,
> We are blest by everything,
> Everything we look upon is blest.

Are we inclined to dismiss this as the fantasy of a light-headed dreamer? Yeats replies,

> Mere dreams, mere dreams! Yet Homer had
>   not sung
> Had he not found it certain beyond dreams
> That out of life's own self-delight had sprung
> The abounding glittering jet . . .

Hero-worship, the heroic view of life seemed desirable to Yeats because through it a man can best come at the abundance of his personality, the full expression of his

own spirit; and "nothing can give dignity to human
nature but the character and energy of its expression." It
is true that, growing older, he questioned the aristocratic
tradition in so far as it is represented by "ancestral houses"
and the culture of the rich:

> now it seems
> As if some marvellous empty sea-shell flung
> Out of the obscure dark of the rich streams,
> And not a fountain, were the symbol which
> Shadows the inherited glory of the rich.

The culture of the Big House had become decadent: its
amenities "But take our greatness with our violence."
Yet the greatness and the violence had not disappeared,
only moved elsewhere:

> An Abbot or Archbishop with an upraised hand
> Blessing the Tricolour. "This is not," I say
> "The dead Ireland of my youth, but an Ireland
> The poets have imagined, terrible and gay."

Just as the heroic view of life gives man images of
virtue, by representing him at his loftiest, most intensely
living moments, so ancestor-worship helps him to discover
his own identity. I take "ancestor-worship" to mean that
feeling of affinity for another person, whether dead or
alive which reveals to a man some truth about himself,
and rouses him to emulation. An ancestor, in this sense,
may be a friend or enemy—the living image of oneself, so
to say, or its extreme opposite. All that matters is the
sense of affinity, and the power it gives us to recognize
our own selves by the intimate identification with
another. A poet's ancestors are those other poets who,
from time to time, provide the medium through which
he can realize a new theme, explore a virgin field of
subject-matter. They are what the literary critic calls
"influences." For Yeats, it was at first William Morris and

Blake. The affinity with Blake proved a lasting one; Morris was displaced—"And I shall dine at journey's end With Landor and with Donne." But Yeats in his poetry celebrated not only these literary ancestors: side by side with Lionel Johnson and "that enquiring man, John Synge," we find the semi-legendary figures of his boyhood —Pollexfens, Middletons, Butlers; friends of later years— Augusta Gregory and her son, MacDonagh and Pearse, Horton, MacGregor and Florence Emery—"All those that manhood tried, or childhood loved Or boyish intellect approved;" even the one or two politicians he admired— O'Leary, Kevin O'Higgins.

All these people linked Yeats with a tradition, helped him to root himself and to gain self-knowledge. The tradition was an aristocratic one. We may discount the exaggerations and the anomalies which Yeats' exuberance attached to this tradition. We shall not agree that all good things come only from the highborn, the peasant or the artist: we know very well that the libertarian ideas which Yeats so distrusted have time and again been forwarded by aristocracy, and that the bourgeois, whom he despised, are now the chief repository of the conservatism he, theoretically, cherished. This is of minor importance. What matters is the core of the tradition that Yeats upheld, not its wrappings. Aristocracy meant for him lofty and daring thought, vivid and passionate action, brimming personality rather than drab and complacent nonentity, independence of mind, courtesy in human relations and style in art—all that is gay, vigorous, proud, magnanimous, self-delighting. Do we wish to reject such a tradition? to measure human dignity by the average rather than by the best? If so, we must tell our poets to celebrate the sheep in sheep's clothing, to render the Common Man's self-esteem more complacent still by praising "the new narcissism of the also-ran."

No, it won't work. Men must always have something to look up to, if they would learn proper pride—that positive whose negative is complacence. Human dignity—which must involve both worthiness and worth-while-ness—feeds on the spirit: there is no mass-produced, patent food which will long substitute for it. Neither dictators nor film stars will do, for in worshipping them men are bowing down before the product of their own mediocrity, the altar of the lowest common denominator. Each of us has a touch of the fine spirit: and this can be made finer only by looking up to the finest spirits of all. Yeats' poetry constantly directs our eyes towards them: this is his will and testament—the estate of the fine, free spirit.

It is time that I wrote my will;
I choose upstanding men
That climb the streams until
The fountain leap, and at dawn
Drop their cast at the side
Of dripping stone; I declare
They shall inherit my pride,
The pride of people that were
Bound neither to Cause nor to State,
Neither to slaves that were spat on
Nor to the tyrants that spat,
The people of Burke and of Grattan
That gave, though free to refuse—
Pride, like that of the morn,
When the headlong light is loose,
Or that of the fabulous horn,
Or that of the sudden shower
When all streams are dry,
Or that of the hour
When the swan must fix his eye
Upon a fading gleam,
Float out upon a long
Last reach of glittering stream
And there sing his last song.